I didn't mean to cause Trouble

SUPERNATURAL STORIES

DR. DAVID R. KITELEY

FOREWORD BY PATRICK D. KITELEY

I Didn't Mean to Cause Trouble: Supernatural Stories

by Dr. David R. Kiteley

Copyright © 2017 by Dr. David R. Kiteley

Published by Kudu Publishing

Print ISBN: 978-1-943294-71-8

I Didn't Mean to Cause Trouble is also available on Amazon Kindle, Barnes & Noble Nook and Apple iBooks.

Endorsements

The author and I, our sons and ministry team have experienced many sovereign open doors where mass miracles of healing, salvation and ministry callings occurred in a number of former Soviet nations in some of the most humorous settings. This book will bring great healing and refreshment to those who are currently laboring and also those who would dare to answer the call of God to labor in the nations of the world.

Bishop Bart Pierce,
Rock City Church, Baltimore

This book will impact and stretch the faith of not only the now generation but also generations to come. Be ready to experience an unusual encounter, which is supernaturally natural and naturally supernatural.

Dr. Paul Tan,
Apostle, City Blessing Churches Int.

Pastor David is a man of truth and has been a friend of mine for many years. I have personally had the privilege of being with him on many occasions experiencing situations both nationally and internationally. We have laughed and cried. I wholeheartedly endorse this book as I have seen David Kiteley face trouble and laugh in its face!

Pastor/Prophet Eric Butler,
Founder of Christian International Church

The reader will experience many modern-day Book of Acts type miraculous accounts. The author has ministered extensively in my country China to thousands of house church leaders as well as in scores of other nations, where God has supernaturally opened doors for him to leave a lasting prophetic impartation.

Dr. Dennis Balcombe, Founding Pastor,
Revival Christian Church in Hong Kong, Apostle to China

I Didn't Mean to Cause Trouble reads much like a contemporary addendum to the Book of Acts, filled with spiritual adventures, faith-filled exploits and enough humor to make the heavens laugh, Psalms 2:4. His courageous inspired apostolic leadership has enriched our lives.

Pastor Dave Bryan,
Church of Glad Tidings, Embassy of Heaven,
Yuba City, California

Pastor David Kiteley has been a voice for the Kingdom of God among the nations. His ministry has left an impact in Japan, not only in our church in Tokyo, but also in many other churches throughout the country. I believe his book, *I Didn't Mean to Cause Trouble*, will impact your life and stir your faith for the miraculous!

Missionary Elmer Inafuku
Senior Pastor of Shinjuku Shalom Church

There is something very powerful and compelling about truly first-hand, eyewitness accounts of the miracle hand of God in the here and now. I have journeyed with David Kiteley for over 30 years and have personally witnessed many of the faith-filled testimonies you are about to read. As you pour over these pages, I believe you will also be inspired to believe God for His miraculous hand in your life!

Doug McClure, Director
YWAM Symphony of Hope International

Contents

Part IV: Overseas Ministry

Dedication

This is dedicated to my wife of 51 years,
Marilyn Grace Kiteley.

To my mother, Dr. Violet Kiteley,
Founder of Shiloh Church,
70+ years of fulltime ministry.

To my son, Pastor Patrick Kiteley,
and his wife, Pastor Marlena Kiteley,
Senior Pastors of Rain Church,
Atlanta, Georgia
and their children, Hailey, Zachary and Hope.

And to my daughter, Pastor Melinda Ramos,
and her husband, Pastor Javier Ramos,
Senior Pastors of Shiloh Church,
Oakland, California
and their children, Joshua and Cristiana.

We have all served together in the ministry
through the challenges and victories,
which made possible all of these
supernatural stories.

Acknowledgements

I WISH TO EXPRESS MY DEEPEST APPRECIATION TO A HOST of dedicated volunteers who assisted me in making the supernatural stories contained in this book come alive.

Special thanks goes to Jon Lew who was the one who initially encouraged and inspired me to get my life stories in print. He spent many hours editing, outlining and organizing the book. To my son, Patrick, who wrote the Foreword and my granddaughter Hailey who designed the cover. Thanks to Rev. Verleeta White who transcribed and formatted the material and also to Sharrié Overall who assisted.

I also appreciate the contributions of Kris Kelley; my daughter, Melinda Ramos, and Ralph and Lori Francis for their proofreading and editing expertise.

Foreword

MY SISTER AND I GREW UP IN A HOME WHERE OUR father told us stories. Those were special times for us. In my memory those moments seem to me as close as last night, yet far away as if they were told a thousand years ago. Many nights, right before bedtime, we would rush in our pajamas to find him to ask this one simple question, "Dad, would you tell us a story?" Being the entertainer, comedian and master storyteller that he was, no matter what he was doing at the time, he would gladly place it to the side to begin yet another story. His stories were sometimes fantastic fictional journeys of characters who would travel to places afar and encounter unusual happenings along the way. Our father has quite the vivid imagination matched with a humorous articulation, which you might have happened to suppose by the thickness of the book you have in hand.

Other times he would tell us stories of people he knew, and let me tell you, he knew some very interesting people. I am talking about people who most would never meet in a lifetime, and he knew more than a hundred of them. It is astonishing to me because somehow he has had an uncanny knack for collecting a remarkable assortment of unique friends and acquaintances in life. So we as children would hear the tales of persons who will go unnamed because you might be reading this book right now. You know who you are! Your hilarious stories made us children laugh and cry at the same time. Thank you for your contribution to our lives, you unnamed friends and family.

For our father laughter was always a part of the equation. Very early on I learned this life principle from him, "If you cannot laugh then you cannot fully live." King Solomon declared it, "Laughter is like a medicine." Laughter heals. Laughter brings life to life. When I look at the friends he has had, I realize that he was always attracted to people who loved to laugh. If you were mad at the world or had a sour demeanor, he probably would love you very much from a distance, but he would not let you into his world of merriment. His penchant for obtaining friends who loved to laugh has shaped my world of friendships in a profound way. What he taught us could be summed in the words of Elizabeth Green, "Sometimes the most ordinary things could be made extraordinary, simply by doing them with the right people."

On most nights though, our father's stories were not fictional fantasies of dragons and knights or about the extraordinary experiences of other people he knew; instead his stories were mostly—his stories. The stories of his life. His life has been supernatural. Along the way there has been mystery and tragedy. Despair and hope. Challenges and triumphs. Losses and victories. Lots of tears and lots of laughter. Reminds me of the third chapter of Ecclesiastes where the contemplative poet leads us into a revelation of life, "To everything there is a season, a time for every purpose under heaven." From there the author goes on to record a list of life moments. Birth. Death. War. Peace. Silence. Speaking. Embracing. Refrain. Mourning. Dancing and so on. This is a book about the supernatural life of David Ray Kiteley, but it is more than just a bunch of stories. It is about how God can take one man with the world against him and use him to change that world.

As you open up the pages of this book, I encourage you to read it in no particular order, to stop and to put it down and to contemplate it, letting God work something within you. Then pick it up again and repeat. This is not a book to race through. It is a book to pace through. Pace yourself. Let God move. I promise your life will be touched as my life has by these supernatural stories.

In grace, Patrick David Kiteley

PART I

Early Life Experiences, Family and Friends

It became abundantly clear early on in life that I certainly was not born with a silver spoon in my mouth. My early childhood experiences gave evidence to the fact that Christianity is not necessarily the charmed life. I discovered that it was highly possible to be deeply wounded and disillusioned from both the pulpit and the pew. God had sovereignly handpicked friends and family to shape my life for future significant global ministry.

This is where my story begins.

CHAPTER 1
Early Life Experiences

PERHAPS ONE OF THE ADVANTAGES OF GETTING OLDER IS that you end up having a broader range of experiences, which gives you a clearer perspective of why your life unfolded the way it did.

You begin to realize that God in His foreknowledge had an unstoppable master plan, which did not just happen by accident or coincidence. You also begin to understand that everything has a way of coming full circle if you let the Lord fight your battles, realizing that He is the God of the second and third chance, and He is undoubtedly much more merciful and forgiving and faithful than we could ever hope to be.

My father was killed three months before I was born. He was an airman on a reconnaissance mission in the Royal Canadian Air Force and died in a fiery air crash within only a few months of his scheduled discharge. He and my mother were planning to continue their ministry together as missionaries to Sierra Leone in West Africa upon his return home.

Mother's testimony was that she was called to ministry when she was 12 years old. When she was water baptized during a Sunday morning service, Aimee Semple McPherson prayed and prophesied over her. She was ordained at 17 years of age and pastored a Chinese church, which was all in preparation for the ministry she would be partnering with in Hong Kong and China. She and my dad married and ministered together. When my dad was killed, her legs became paralyzed because of trauma. They had been married one year to the day.

At the age of two and a half, I was placed in the Sharon Star Orphanage, which was on the grounds where the 1948 Revival took place in North Battleford, Saskatchewan, Canada. There is a story about a revival service that took place there. When I was three, I prayed for a paralyzed man, and he came out of his wheelchair.

I spent a great deal of time serving on skid row in Vancouver with my mother and grandfather when I was between the ages of five and ten years. They served there up to seven nights a week. There I witnessed my first murder when I was only six years old. I served a turkey dinner at a mission at Christmas to a man who became irate and threw the meal back in my face, and some of the other men present at the dinner threw him from the third floor to his death.

My mother trained many missionaries and ministers, some who had been delivered from alcohol and drug addiction and some who were receiving on-the-job training. She had a unique calling for stirring up the gifts in others, even those who seemed hopeless.

I was raised in a rather legalistic church and learned many things not to do. The old school methods included rapping knuckles, whipping us, forcing us to pray at the top of our lungs with our hands lifted and never allowing us to look down in the prayer room because that was where the devil was. We were encouraged not to leave the long meetings lest we miss something and were told we would never grow up because Khrushchev would bury us. They told us that we would never finish school or get married. The church was planning on storing groceries underground and putting in gas tanks and utilities in preparation for the coming tribulation. On the other hand, they believed that each of us had a calling we needed to fulfill. I answered the mission call every Sunday night for different nations. God took me at my word, and I am still traveling.

My mom, with the support of my grandparents and me, opened a church called Revival Tabernacle in September 1955. This storefront church also served as our accommodations. We lived in a Sunday school room, and I slept on a rollaway on the platform. When a major ministry event or deliverance services took place at that location, I had to wait until the long services were over before I could get to sleep.

In 1958, Revival Tabernacle purchased and moved into a church building on 104th Avenue in Surrey, British Columbia. The basement served as our living quarters, a one-room apartment with no heat except a wood cookstove, and no shower. We used the church restrooms, and I slept on a cot in the Sunday school room. We had no closet and no furniture. In the basement below ground it was pretty cold in winter. Critics often referred to the church as the "Hallelujah Barn" because of testimonies of people traveling a great distance to worship and receive ministry there.

We sent our first missionary to Sierra Leone, which was where my mom and dad had intended to go. There was a miracle of a woman who was dying and had asked her husband to bring her to our church to receive prayer for healing. When the Lord miraculously healed her, her husband was angry because his plans for the life insurance benefit were ruined. I became the target of his anger; he actually hired men to attack me as a means of trying to force our family out of town. I was physically injured, and my shoulder was dislocated.

Following that attack, when I was 13, my mom sent me to live in another city for safety. Since we did not have a lot of money, I stayed with drunks in a basement apartment and paid my rent with a paper route earning $15 a month.

As church members would come for assistance with various needs, my mom often gave away all of our groceries, emptying our fridge. However, I learned to be a believer, as better groceries came later. God always sent others to meet our needs.

In 1964, Revival Tabernacle's Trustee Board elected to remove my mom from her role as senior pastor of the church that she had started and had worked to pay off the mortgage. She had never received a salary or benefits of any kind. The board felt that, as men, they could do a much better job in pastoring the church. Regrettably, a large church in the region encouraged this decision at the time. They supported the board in having my mother removed. Most of this occurred behind the scenes.

I was 19 years of age and very angry and disillusioned. Many of our friends and the congregation turned against us. We moved to another city, and my mother was understandably very upset by the undeserved accusations and ultimate dismissal. I was doing what I could to help her and to mitigate the emotional upset when I met some people from Oakland through my job. They wanted my mom to come and teach at their church.

I knew I needed to get my mom out of the area to start a new life, and we proceeded to get our visas and green cards. Marilyn and I were secretly engaged at the time, but I could not tell my mom, or she would not have been willing to go to Oakland at that time.

My mom's teaching was so powerful that the ministry in Oakland that invited her felt threatened. This was around 1965. She met people from Marin County, Fremont, San Leandro and San Francisco. She started Bible studies throughout the Bay Area. In September 1965, we started Shiloh Church in an African-American home with about 20 people. Shiloh would never have begun had we not been driven out of our church in Surrey. We had never planned to leave Canada nor had any desire to leave Canada.

Miracle after miracle occurred in the new Shiloh Church. The Oakland congregation was representative of the Bay

Area community at that time in history. The Jesus Movement among the hippie community was in full swing. The Charismatic Movement, Civil Rights Movement and other interracial events that people talk about today all had their genesis in the Bay Area. Shiloh was birthed out of all these various and diverse movements. Shiloh sent out missionaries when we were still a very small church to regions like Africa, India, Hong Kong, China, Philippines, Israel and Japan, and supported a Bible College in Myanmar (Burma) during our 50+ years of ministry.

In 1966, Marilyn and I were married and moved back to Canada three months later. One of the greatest miracles was that we returned at the age of 22 to pastor the church that my mother and family had been kicked out of. Talk about things going full circle! God brought great restoration and healing. My mother was even able to come back several times to minister. Incidentally the church is still going strong 61 years later as a Foursquare Church with a thousand members. What God plants remains, regardless of the shaking. During our time of pastoring and serving in Surrey, Marilyn and I became foster parents of two boys, who are now in their 60s. In 1970, my mom was afflicted with cancer, and I was called to return with Marilyn to pastor Shiloh Church in Oakland. People in our church in Canada thought we would just be taking a leave of absence and would return. But we have been in Oakland ever since. I became the co-pastor and ministered every other Sunday, and eventually became the senior pastor.

Humor in Ministry
WHY MY GRANDFATHER LIVED TO 105 YEARS OF AGE

My grandfather was born on February 23, 1883 in an Indian village on Manitoulin Island, a Canadian island in Lake Huron. His

21

family members were the first European settlers on the island. He lived to the ripe old age of 105 and died on June 19, 1988.

At 99 years of age, he took his first two aspirin and then phoned me to come to him so he could tell me that he had sinned. He said, "You are my pastor, and I would understand if you and the elders of the church felt led to put me out of the church for taking drugs." He said, "I have prayed for hundreds of people who were addicted to drugs and alcohol, and then slapped them on the mouth and said, 'Never again!'" He got tremendous results as he prayed the prayer of faith over them. He said, "I am so ashamed, but today I had the first headache that I have ever had in my life and, rather than believe God for my healing, I resorted to taking drugs myself."

I said, "Grandpa, no worries. God will forgive you, and if we kicked you out of the church for taking aspirin, we would probably have to close the church altogether because everyone in the congregation has more than likely taken pain pills many times over."

Grandpa had a special diet of MacDonald's hamburgers and Church's fried chicken. He liked Church's chicken, french fries and classic Coke, which he would eat and drink every day, if he could get someone to take him to the fast food restaurant. We told him, on a number of occasions, that he should eat more healthy foods like salads, but his reply was, "Salads are not good for you; they are rabbits' food." He would go on to say that he used to be a farmer and had hundreds of rabbits on his land and the life expectancy of a rabbit was two years. He also said that eating carrots does not improve your eyesight. That is a myth and simply not true because he saw all kinds of dead rabbits along the roadways because they could not see the oncoming cars. He finally agreed that if he ate salads, he might live six months longer. Then he added that when he died he would not have a smile on his face in his coffin. It would make people feel very sad or even scared when they viewed his remains. His long life was certainly not the result of his love for junk food; he got away with it, but we are not recommending it for anyone except maybe on rare occasions.

My grandfather received his Doctorate of Theology degree when he was 100 years old. He had been faithfully attending the Bible College for 25 years. He said it may have taken him a whole lot longer than most, but at least he finally got it.

We bought him a new large print Bible when he was 100. He took off his reading glasses, smashed them on the ground and began shouting, "Hallelujah, I am healed!" and he refused to ever wear them again. We did not have the heart to tell him that the reason he could suddenly read the Bible without glasses was the large print.

His long life was the result of loving God and loving people. His greatest joy was to be in a red-hot worship service. He told me that he never wanted to be in an old people's home; he wanted to be where there was life and joy and laughter. The thing that irritated him the most was when he saw young people who looked old.

My grandfather rarely seemed stressed out; he believed in practicing the scripture that states, "A merry heart doeth good like a medicine." He was still praying for the sick, right up until two days before he died. He was hardly sick a day in his life. The morning he died, he got up, shaved, put on his suit and sat back in his chair, and his heart just stopped. He never took himself too seriously, nor did he believe in worry. His good sense of humor kept him alive and healthy a lot longer than most of his contemporaries.

Humor in Ministry
SEEKER-FRIENDLY CHURCHES

In recent years one of the newest and fastest-growing movements within evangelical churches has been referred to as the seeker-sensitive or seeker-friendly movement. These churches offer more informal services that are usually much shorter, much more entertaining and less intimidating. Subjects like denying oneself, forsaking all others to follow Christ, repentance and sin are not often addressed because they do not fit very well with their marketing brand. They claim that the most positive factor of their church is that they are reaching thousands of non-believers with a message that initially deals with people's felt needs as well as improving the quality of their day-to-day lives. They state that this is the hook that gets them in the door so that they can later, through mid-week services and home meetings, hopefully become converted.

This method seems to be working exceptionally well for them, as growing megachurches are springing up all across the nation. And this concept is being exported around the world, even though the primary purpose and call of the New Testament church is found in Ephesians 4:11-13 and is to mature and equip the saints so that they in turn can be sent out to reach the lost within their sphere of influence. Nevertheless, we laud and applaud the seeker-friendly churches as being a first step church to reach people who probably never would have been touched by God. Paul admonishes us in Philippians 1 to always rejoice when Christ is preached even if we may not prefer the methodology that is utilized.

As I was thinking about this topic of seeker-friendly churches, my mind went back to a rather humorous incident that occurred when I was five years of age. This was decades before the term seeker-friendly or seeker-sensitive was ever conceived.

My kindergarten teacher requested that I escort two East Indian pre-teen boys who were my neighbors to school each day. They were newly landed immigrants who spoke very little English, and the school leaders decided to put them in kindergarten for a couple of weeks so that they could learn the basics. One day these young men asked me to go with them to their Indian Sikh church, which had a daily afterschool noon service.

When we arrived at the church, I was asked to join the orchestra, and they gave me some simple percussion instruments and told me that I could sit up in the orchestra section in the front with my new friends. I went home and told my mom that I had found a new very friendly church. I told her that I wanted to continue to go there and that I had been asked to be part of the orchestra, which is something that our church would never allow a five-year-old to do.

My mother, who was a Pentecostal Holiness-type preacher, was totally horrified when she discovered that her five-year-old son wanted to join an Indian Sikh church, but at least she had to admit that it was "Sikher" and kid-friendly. Still, she forbade me to go to their noon services.

Decades later the shoe was on the other foot, and a woman from this same Sikh religion came to the church where I was raised. She suffered from stage four cancer and came as a last resort. Our church believed and practiced prayer for divine healing accompanied by the laying on of hands. As the story goes, she was totally healed and received Jesus Christ as her Lord and Savior. A few weeks later, she returned back to this church, along with a large contingency of East Indians from the Sikh church. They had heard the report from her doctor that her cancer had gone into remission. When the altar call was given for salvation, these visiting Sikhs all came forward to receive Jesus because they discovered that the good news of God was not just being proclaimed, but that it actually worked. This is what I call a true "Sikher-friendly" service.

CHAPTER 2

A True Servant, Pastor Violet Kiteley

IN HIS BOOK *SPIRITUAL LEADERSHIP* J. OSWALD SANDERS says that the term "leader" is used only six times in the entire Bible, three times in the singular and three times in the plural. However, there are hundreds of Christian books written on the subject of leadership.[1] The majority of them contain a considerable amount of principles developed by corporate America with a few biblical references and examples thrown in. The number one qualification for biblical leadership in the New Testament is that of being a servant.

Servanthood is one of the *least* sought-after positions found in every era of human history. The whole notion of the Philippians 2 model, which refers to taking on the form of a servant and making yourself of no reputation, seems rather archaic, especially in a society where proper imaging and marketing appear to be mandatory if you desire to be a so-called success.

In Jeremiah 45:5, the prophet asks a rather probing question, "Are you seeking great things for yourself?" Then he gives the admonition, "Do not seek them." The world is not suffering for lack of Christian celebrities, and too many normal regular

---

1. *Spiritual Leadership,* J. Oswald Sanders, 1967 The Moody Bible Institute

believers have become inactive and shifted all sense of the responsibility to these so-called superstars. We need people who not only know how to preach the tenets of the restoration message, but who actually become restorers and reconcilers for people who have fallen and feel that they have blown it beyond repair. These are people who know how to throw out a lifeline, and are even willing to be disapproved of and misunderstood in order to see others lifted up and restored. Their ultimate goal is to see the Kingdom of God advanced and succeed beyond themselves.

Such was the life and ministry of my mother, Dr. Violet Kiteley, who passed on to her eternal reward on Thanksgiving Day, 2015. She was a true servant leader whose influence extended far beyond her watch as a pastor, Bible College president and worldwide anointed prophetic preacher. Each generation of her family, from her children to her grandchildren and great-grandchildren, specifically benefited and learned valuable lessons from her life, which fully demonstrated what she preached.

My mother was a rare breed, who was 100 percent sold on and totally serious about the work of God. I never remember her ever taking a day off or going on a vacation with me while I was growing up. She did not believe in engaging in small talk and had little or no use for sports or for shopping. She never went to a theater and the only television that she watched was *The 700 Club*. She obviously was not your normal parent. She embraced challenging scriptures that said, unless you are willing to forsake father, mother, and children or houses and land for the Lord's sake then you cannot be His disciple.

Many ministers told her that it was virtually impossible in this modern society to follow her rigid example, to which she invariably answered, "That is a matter between me and God." She would say, "Let me be who God has called me to be, and I will extend the same grace toward you."

Throughout her ministry she was always willing to embrace the unwanted and the unlovely and individuals who did not smell, act or look right, according to other people's standards, whether it was flower children from Haight-Ashbury in San Francisco, hippies from Berkeley or derelicts on skid row in urban cities. She always related to people from other races and other cultures before doing so became popular. In fact, in years gone by, it was generally frowned upon. She often laid hands on inebriated people in public venues, even out in the streets, and prayed them through to sobriety before she would lead them to the Lord.

My mother was no respecter of persons and was effective in ministering to people from any status of life, whether they were from the margins of urban Oakland, or more affluent, well-educated professionals from Marin County. She treated them all the same as if they were God's special, chosen people. She believed that they were all on an equal playing field and regularly went to minister in their homes for Bible studies without intimidation.

My mother and I marched for the Civil Rights Movement in the mid-60s. We firmly believed that it was a movement of God, even though some of the politicians tried to co-opt the movement for their own political agendas. To her it was a matter of righteousness, equity and social justice. She always preached that racism was a sin and needed to be repented of, and totally eradicated from any church or ministry that called themselves Christian.

After emigrating from Canada in the mid-60s, our ministry in the Bay Area was initially misunderstood and opposed by some white and black churches until they finally realized that we were not into grandstanding or getting on a new faddish soapbox, but sincerely believing in racial reconciliation. God had planted us in the Bay Area, and we were there to stay and to be a blessing to everybody.

One of the highlights of Pastor Violet Kiteley's ministry was that she was fully committed to raising up spiritual leadership and missionaries who responded positively to her anointed teaching gift as well as her sacrificial lifestyle. She had a God-given ability to inspire and motivate people to discover and lay hold of their placement in the Body of Christ.

My mother was always willing to minister in a small church that could hardly afford to give her gas money, let alone an offering. Yet she never, ever complained, and she taught her family, as I did, that God is our paymaster, not the church. She often would say, "They don't own me—God does." She poured out to people generously and never expected payment from anyone. Over the years, there were those who felt she was an easy mark and would go directly to her home after hours requesting financial aid for electric bills, phone bills, rent and car repairs as well as a lot of non-essentials. They would go to her directly if they did not want to deal with the church benevolence board because that would mean that there would have to be some accountability.

For a number of years, the church board and the congregation would attempt to raise her meager salary at the annual business meeting, but she would then get up and immediately decline it, and would say something to the effect that the money could be better used for outreach and missions, which was her passion. My mother also firmly believed that real servanthood ministry could only take place when someone was willing to serve on their own personal time after hours. She believed that, as long as you were being paid for everything you did, that you had already received your reward. Consequently, she believed in tithing of your time as well as your money. I remember, on a number of occasions, when people were waiting on jobs to come through that they had applied for months before. She would tell them that these jobs would not materialize until they were willing to serve the church free of charge for a season. Numerous unemployed individuals were hired for good paying positions *after* they embraced this principle and volunteered their time for a season to the house of God. She believed that we were all called to function from a servant's throne.

My mother was always the first one to visit the bedside of one who was gravely ill or was facing challenging life circumstances, whether it was in their house or at the hospital. It did not matter what time of day or night it was. She understood that you needed to be constantly prayed up and have your full armor on because you never knew the moment you would be called into service. She also firmly believed that the power of life and death was in the power of the tongue. She never wanted to hang around negative people. She believed that it was a sin to spend time with people who did not choose to change after a long season of grace. It was vital to her that people understood that she could not be their shepherd if they were not receptive to her ministry.

She had an uncanny ability to remember everyone's name after she met them for the first time. She would personally take roll call every Sunday even though the church had hundreds of people in each service. If someone missed church for any reason, they would receive a bulletin with a personal handwritten note in it. Recently, an Oakland pastor told me that he had visited my mother's church several years back. He filled out a visitor's card, and one of the questions was the date of his birthday. He said that resulted in his receiving a birthday card for the next 15 years. Having attended a different church for decades, where leadership still didn't know his name, he was impressed with her ability to be highly relational.

My mother made it her business to attempt to stay in touch with ministers and missionaries all over the world on a regular basis. Unfortunately, many of them whom she poured out her life for often did not put out near the level of diligence to staying in contact with her. Sad to say, my mother was often overlooked at large conferences and would frequently sit by herself in the front row, praying before the meeting, even though she was the principle speaker. The church elite would all gather in the back in the conference green room for a brief fellowship session. When she finally was introduced and got up to speak and the anointing of God was released upon the gathered, attitudes changed. The very same people who failed to acknowledge her earlier began flocking around her at the end of the service, which she did not particularly care for. A notable individual in national ministry stated that though he did not believe in female ministers per se, he had to conclude and declare that Pastor Violet Kiteley was the real deal. He stated that he particularly appreciated the fact that she did not attempt to act like a man or be pushy or overbearing and "knew her place."

This was often not the case among many insecure female ministers in the past. My mother never really cared too much about what people thought of her personally. When she prayed for a person, it was usually short and to the point. If you needed correction, she gave you correction; if you needed encouragement, she gave you encouragement. She always knew her limitations and tried to stay within her own lane and often called in other ministries from the team to take over if prolonged ministry was required, e.g., extended deliverance sessions.

On one occasion a few years back, she started to feel very faint and actually passed out during a staff meeting. We called an ambulance and rushed her to a hospital. After the initial tests, they decided that they wanted to admit her. The only way we as a family could convince her to agree to being admitted was to tell her that we would set up a rotational schedule of pastors to come to the hospital so that she could teach them from the Word. Otherwise, she was going home because it would be a total waste of time to lie around in the hospital.

During the last few years of her life, she prayed strong prophetic prayers and gave accurate words of knowledge and direction to people she did not recognize because she was suffering from dementia. This gave a whole lot more validity to the prophetic realm than when someone has prior knowledge about the individual they are ministering to.

We wrote on her tombstone that she was a once-in-a-lifetime prophetic voice who left her imprint on all the lives she touched around the world. Dr. Violet Kiteley was indeed a true servant.

CHAPTER 3

Rev. Leora Overall—A Spiritual Mother

O UR HOME CHURCH IS DISTINCTIVELY BLESSED TO have foundational families and faithful members who have attended the ministry for more than four decades. They have possessed an unwavering faith throughout all the mountaintop victories and challenging valley experiences of doing life together in a body setting.

Their legacy is one of continuing to contend for the fulfillment of all the prophetic words that have gone over the house throughout the years concerning personal and corporate breakthrough and revival. This is not normal today in America, particularly in an urban, mobile society, for anyone to have children, grandchildren and great-grandchildren all regularly attending and actively participating in the same church with the matriarch of their family during a span of over 45 years.

Rev. Leora Overall is a true spiritual mother to hundreds of congregants, both young and old, who affectionately call her "Wowa" (pronounced "Whoa wah"), including her six children, 21 grandchildren and 23 great-grandchildren, with undoubtedly many more to come.

Her special love and compassion for children and their families has caused her to be instrumental in bringing about household salvation, as well as impartational prayer to receive the baptism of the Holy Spirit. She has released and activated teaching and prophetic gifts into the life of various ministries in the church.

My children, Patrick and Melinda, as well as scores of other children of all races, have adopted her as their grandma, remembering how she taught them to read and instilled in them love for the Word of God. Whether it was teaching children or adults in the Bible college, or directing the Rest Home or Seniors Ministry or being a chaplain at Highland County Hospital, she was always a bright and shining light.

Rev. Leora always radiated the joy of the Lord even in the most trying situations. She would rise up quickly and rebound after a time of personal bereavement. She has been a woman with a word of wisdom and a strong gift of discernment. She has been a friend, encourager and counselor to numerous churches and pastors who were going through a particularly difficult season and desperately needed to hear a word from the Lord.

Leora was a close friend, confidante, traveling companion and spiritual protectorate to my late mother, Dr. Violet Kiteley, as they traveled in ministry to China, Ethiopia, Israel, Japan, Jamaica and all over America and parts of Canada together. She would sing, prophesy and intercede as well as be the PR person for the various conferences that she and my mother were teamed in ministry for.

Bishops, pastors and church leaders usually invited them to come together, as they viewed them as one package in united ministry and covenant sisters. Leora Overall is an irreplaceable part of the lives of the Kiteley and Ramos families. We love and honor her and have been greatly enriched by "Wowa," our spiritual mother.

Humor in the Ministry
THROWING UP IN THE PULPIT

My mother, Pastor Violet, firmly believed and preached that the word "can't" is not to be found anywhere in the Bible. She traveled extensively, ministering in the Pacific Northwest, and took me with her during the summers. She had a compelling desire to get me up behind the pulpit to become a preacher, perhaps because I was her only child. When I was six, she would give me a verse and a topic, usually on the subject of revival, and tell me that I needed to speak for five to ten minutes.

I would normally attempt to say something that made some sense even though for the most part I did not have a clue what I was talking about. Although people were very encouraging and thought I was very cute, I never enjoyed doing it, and would shake like a leaf, fearful of standing up before a crowd.

In my early teens, my mother arranged for me to preach a whole message in her weekly Friday night service. I prepared literally for weeks, and the more I studied, the more I was convinced that there was no way that I could do it and was dreading the night. On that eventful night, when I got up to speak, I was so upset to my stomach that I literally threw up over the pulpit. The people did not know whether to laugh or cry. I ran out of the building where my mother followed me, telling me to clean up and get back in the pulpit and finish the message that I had not even started.

I told her I had absolutely nothing to say, and furthermore, I did not even want to be there. She knew that if she let me off the hook, I would probably never, ever be willing to minister again. She said something that was very amusing, even though I knew she hadn't thought it out before she said it. She quoted a Bible verse that said, "Just open your mouth and the Lord will fill it." I told her I had already done that and look what happened. We both laughed and that helped to break the ice. Looking back, I am glad I was not let off the hook, as painful as it was, or I may not be in the ministry today.

CHAPTER 4

The Pastor's Wife and Family

IN DAYS GONE BY, THE PASTOR'S WIFE, PARTICULARLY IN A small church, was often as carefully scrutinized as her husband when a church board was in the process of selecting a new minister to fill the vacant pulpit. The traditional expectation was that she would be a multi-talented individual with a vibrant personality, who could effectively reach out and be accepted by people of all ages. She needed to play the piano, sing solos for special occasions, oversee the office, prepare the weekly bulletin, organize and cook for all fellowship offerings, visit the sick and shut-ins, oversee the nursery, teach women's and children's classes and do anything that was needed whenever there was no one else available. She was always expected to possess a good attitude, be a social butterfly and receive what other people thought as constructive criticism graciously. Not to mention the fact that she was expected to have an exemplary family life with a good marriage and exceptionally well-behaved, polite children. She also needed to have ample time for herself to maintain an exercise routine and have a strong intercessory devotional life. Of course, all of this was with the understanding that she and her husband would come as one package and that his low to moderate salary would be more than enough for the both of them. After all, as far as the church boards in times past were concerned, this was considered to be sacrificial ministry that possessed its own eternal reward.

They didn't often consider that the pastor's home has the same kind of responsibility and bills that everyone else had. This was the kind of life my gracious wife, Marilyn, unbeknownst to her, was called to partner in when she agreed to marry me over five decades ago!

We met January 1, 1962, both of us at the tender age of 16, while skating on a frozen pond in Canada. We literally fell for each other. Marilyn's parents had a traditional Lutheran background and were extremely concerned that their eldest daughter might be getting involved in a cult-like church. She had been attending our church four nights a week and all-day Sunday and returning home late at night. This was extremely worrisome to them. Not to mention the fact that she was now dating the son of the pastor who happened to be a woman, which was something extremely foreign to them at the time. Marilyn was the first one in her family to be born again, and she earnestly prayed for her family for over 35 years. She firmly believed in Acts 16:31, which makes reference to household salvation. She was blessed to see her whole family come into the Kingdom of God, beginning with her siblings. Her brother, Chris, came to the church we pastored in Surrey. Karen, her sister, received the Lord and was baptized in the Holy Spirit and married a minister from the Bay Area. Her youngest sister, Leanne [now in heaven], and her whole family also came to know the Lord. Her father, mother and grandmother in their latter years had personal experiences with Jesus. This is a testament to the fact that prayer works.

Marilyn and I came from two totally different backgrounds. I think that the thing that first attracted me to her was her easygoing, hang loose, infectious laugh and contagious joy, which she still possesses to this day. I can often find her in a large store just by listening for her laugh, as she is carrying on an in-depth conversation with someone she has just met a few minutes before. On the other hand, I come from a much more rigid background, where we weren't nearly as outwardly expressive but tended to be more serious and stoic and even at times, poker-faced. This was true even though we were usually very content and peaceful on the inside. God knows who each of us needs in order to provide us with the balance and replenishment that is so desperately needed, particularly in ministry.

At 19 years of age we were engaged, and we were separated for about a year and a half because my mother was literally forced out of the church she pioneered. This separation served to test the validity of our relationship.

I had specifically told Marilyn that I would never under any circumstances become a pastor. I was a firsthand eyewitness of what ministry entailed, and it was far too costly and demanding for my liking. I told her I wanted to have a totally different type of life for my future family and myself. However, I learned quickly to never say never because a year and a half later, at 22 years of age, we were senior pastors in the same church my mother had founded. Many people in the small congregation were twice our age. This was a huge adjustment for both of us but especially for my wife, who knew little or nothing about what a minister's life would entail.

A pastor's wife has a very significant role to fulfill in the church. She must support her man even when she is not totally convinced that the direction he has taken is the best course of action. She must try to support him in every season whether celebrating on the mountaintops of victory or dealing with the disappointments in the valleys. I used to keep a letter of resignation in the top drawer of my desk. For the first few years of ministry, I pulled it out every Monday just to read it. It brought comfort to me; if it didn't work, there was a way out. Marilyn had to talk me out of resigning, so that I could just hang in there for another week. Marilyn not only performed all the duties of a wife in a small church but was y biggest cheerleader and "amen" corner in the pew. She also was my sounding board. She listened to me practice my messages and gave me suggestions. She laughed at my corny jokes even though she had heard them a number of times before. And they honestly were not that funny, especially the canned ones.

She finally got up enough nerve in the last few years to tell me she had not been totally truthful when she stated in the early days of our ministry how great my messages were. She said, "They really weren't all that good, but it has taken me decades to finally get enough nerve to tell you just how bad they really were compared to your messages now."

Marilyn told me many years later how often she had felt inadequate and insignificant in ministry, and it seemed that there was always some plant of the enemy to make her feel that way. For example, a woman prayed over her and said in her prayer that she couldn't believe how bad Marilyn must feel because she doesn't have the same gifts that my mother had to preach and prophesy. However, Marilyn told me how the Lord has always been faithful, even in those kinds of times, to drop a word into her Spirit, that she was only to be who God called her to be, nothing more and nothing less. The Lord specifically told her that she doesn't need to line up to anyone else's expectations or standards but to stay in her own lane. She was never called to compete with anyone else. Nor was she to be compared with any other shiny female ministry examples.

The Lord saw fit for us to foster two teenage boys in our homes at different times, who happened to be less than ten years younger than us. Both of them taught us valuable lessons that we were able to utilize in our future pastoral ministry, as well as when we had our own biological children.

The first foster child placed with us was very devious. He would buy airplane glue to supposedly make plastic models; however, the truth of it was he was sniffing the glue to get high. He would steal our car in the night and go out joy riding, coming back with an empty tank. He was extremely manipulative, especially with women, which is why he had been in 13 homes prior to coming to us. Marilyn has always been a very discerning straight shooter and was often able to see things clearly before I was. We found out that his behavior had the potential to divide our home and marriage. We came into agreement to bind that manipulative spirit, and God placed him into another home.

Our second foster son was an intelligent young businessman who went to school daily in a three-piece suit, carried a briefcase and refused to socialize with the kids in his class because he thought they were too immature. However, he would utilize a number of them to go door-to-door selling plaster of Paris plaques that he made. Oftentimes he had much more money than Marilyn and I did. His zealousness to preach the gospel often angered school staff. On one occasion, he corrected the teacher and asked her to take her seat in the classroom during a lesson in which she was drawing an Easter bunny on the blackboard. He went up and erased it, and then drew three crosses and explained what Easter was really all about. This resulted in Marilyn being called to the school. When all the children caught a glimpse of her, they asked him, "How come your mom looks so young?" to which he replied, "I'm sorry that your mothers look so old." All of these things presented us great opportunities to teach him what grace and mercy were all about. Although he was doing the right thing, he was doing it in the wrong manner. He loved God deeply, and we would have brought him to the United States when we moved here permanently in 1970, if it weren't for the fact that the Vietnam War was going on. He would have been drafted within a few years.

A few years later we had two precious children, Patrick and Melinda. This was during the tumultuous 70s with *Roe vs. Wade*, the Watergate scandal and all the unrest and turmoil on university campuses over the Vietnam conflict, not to mention the free love, emerging drug culture and the hippie movement, mostly originating in the San Francisco Bay Area where we lived. It appeared that time-honored institutions as well as traditional American values were being challenged and changed forever. One could not help but wonder what kind of unsettled world we were birthing our children into. All we could do was conclude that God must have a special calling on their generation, and we groomed and nurtured them with the utmost of care.

My wife had read stories about John Wesley, founder of the Methodist movement, and his mother, Susanna, who had given birth to 19 children. She asked God when they were very young to give her specific insights concerning the individual talents or gifts of each of her children. This would give her the ability to try to provide the resources and training necessary to make them successful in their future life. My wife taught our children the importance of doing everything with the spirit of excellence so that whatever their hands find to do, to do it with all their heart. She instilled in them the fact that they each had their own unique gift capacity, and their only goal should be to try to reach their own potential. She told them that God's people always deserved the very best, which she demonstrated generously, even when we didn't have a lot of extras ourselves. She would shop at the second-hand store, bargain hunt, clip coupons, grind wheat, bake bread and pies and make meals from scratch. This was always with the thought of trying to teach our children the value of money. Our house was often filled with friends and even strangers, especially during holidays when Patrick would bring home anyone he came in contact with who didn't have a place to go. They would eat up everything in sight. He would often leave them with us and go off with his friends. Marilyn would have to go to Costco the next day to replenish our refrigerator.

Our daughter Melinda had a very strong passion for children. She became an assistant Sunday school teacher at the age of 12. After obtaining her college degree, she taught kindergarten for one year and was so successful that three of her students later skipped a grade due to the strong foundation she gave them, particularly in reading where they were several grades ahead of their classmates. Melinda, like her father, had stated that she never desired to be in pastoral ministry because she too knew firsthand just how hard it was and stated that it was not the career path she'd chosen for her life. We told both of our children on numerous occasions that we strongly preferred that they never pursue ministry. The only qualifications would be if they were 100 percent certain that God had called them and that it was not due to the will of any man. We told the congregation publicly from the pulpit on a number of occasions to not put pressure on them concerning ministry. Obviously, God had other plans for both of them.

We are delighted to say that Melinda served as a highly successful children's ministry pastor for 20 years. Her husband, Pastor Javier Ramos, joined her as a partner in ministry. At one point, they were serving hundreds of children in various children's outreach ministries, including sidewalk Sunday school on public school property or in adjoining parks.

In 2015, Javier and Melinda Ramos were set in as senior pastors at Shiloh Church where our daughter's teaching and administrative gifts totally complement her husband's pastoral anointing. He has a high degree of energy and is bi-vocational, with an educational background in molecular biology. He works as a supervisor in our local water company as well as serves as a pastor. His primary vision is to equip individuals to function outside of the four walls of the church. Our grandkids Joshua and Cristiana and their children also have a heart for the ministry of the house, and they regularly serve in various capacities where they make the church their second home. Joshua has a special calling in worship and sings and plays the piano. Cristiana has leadership qualities much like her mother and is already leading children.

Our son, Patrick, officially became full-time staff at age 20 and served as a college career pastor. He pioneered Impact, which was an outreach ministry to students at the University of California, Berkeley, and other campuses. He later became the co-pastor, with his wife Marlena, in 2008. Marlena has a gift of hospitality, and a strong gift for supportive behind-the-scenes work. She even preaches on occasion. They served as senior pastors for eight years, during which time hundreds of people were saved and added to the church. He and his family have recently planted a multicultural church named "Rain" in Atlanta, Georgia. Within six months of launching the ministry, they were able to lease a building, and have just broken the hundred-attendance mark. Patrick travels extensively and has a strong preaching prophetic mantle. Many notable miracles take place in conferences where he has been called to minister.

Our granddaughter Hailey has a powerful worship ministry, which consists of writing original songs, leading worship, recording, and singing on national television, as well as having her own ministry of outreach to the pop culture.

Our grandson Zach is a very creative thinker and wants to pursue a business career so he can financially support the house of God. He is very zealous to see the church grow and has a real servant's heart. Our youngest grandchild is Hope, who has been a tremendous strength and encouragement to the family with her upbeat and joyful disposition.

We are extremely delighted to see how both our children's families are currently functioning in covenant ministry in their respective churches at both ends of the country. I give my wife a huge amount of credit for being a truly exemplary model of what real, unpretentious Christian ministry is all about. Marilyn has had to take a lesser role through most of our entire ministry life. She never tried to compete for the first lady position, due to my mother Pastor Violet's strong gifting. Even though it was rightfully hers during the 22 years of functioning as a senior pastor, she was willing to take a lesser role and be comfortable in the place God had chosen for her without complaint. My wife was the glue that held our family together in the midst of manifold pressures and un-warranted criticism. I told her on numerous occasions, "You are not the wife of the church. You are my wife, and there is nothing about you that I desire to change." My wife is truly a God-pleaser, not a man-pleaser, and that is why we are still together and going strong after 50+ years of marriage.

Humor in Ministry

ANSWERING EMERGENCIES

It was our first Christmas in our new pastorate in Surrey, British Columbia, when I received an emergency call from a stranger by the name of Hank. I had been thoroughly trained that if you were a minister and if someone ever used the word "emergency," it was an equivalent to 911. This meant that it was time to rush out the door immediately. My wife was going all out to prepare a very special celebratory meal for this annual occasion. She was totally startled as I used the password, "emergency," and hurriedly kissed her and told her to just go ahead and eat, as I had no idea when I would be returning. She told me later that she could only imagine that someone had been in a serious car accident or had perhaps even died. She was trying to be understanding concerning the level of trauma that I must have been experiencing at that moment. Hank had given me an address that I did not readily recognize. I later discovered that it was the Turf Hotel, a popular 24-hour watering hole for hardened alcoholics. When I arrived at the hotel and found the guy, he was pretty much inebriated, and he was crying like a baby. He told me that his wife no longer wanted him and was ready to file for divorce. During the process of trying to minister to him, I asked him how long he had been separated from his wife. He stated that it had been about a couple of months. I knew at that moment that I had been taken big time and that the only emergency that was happening at that moment was back at our home where my wife was preparing our Christmas meal. Hank then asked me to drive him over to the house to talk with his wife. When we arrived, Hank went up and knocked at the door; the man who opened the door asked us what we were doing there. Hank stated that he had come to visit his wife. The guy yelled at us to leave the property, because, he said, "I have been her new husband for over three years," and he was ready to call the police because we were trespassing on his property.

Hank then asked me to drive him to the Salvation Army shelter, which was several miles away, where they were unable to admit him until he sobered up. Finally, they agreed to let him sit in the lobby and drink strong coffee and even sleep in one of the chairs if he didn't have any other options. When I finally made it home, it was almost dark, and the food had already been put away in the fridge for tomorrow's leftovers. Explaining this emergency 911 trip wasn't all that easy, but finally my wife agreed to forgive me. I promised to make sure that it was a true emergency before I ran off chasing some unknown stranger who was inebriated in a bar, particularly on Christmas.

Humor in Ministry

$2,500 ANNIVERSARY DINNER

Anniversary dinners and getaways are very special events that should be reserved exclusively for the one who has chosen to walk through life with you. Even after 51 years of marriage, my wife still looks forward for several weeks to our anniversary, and would like to make it a weeklong celebration if possible.

A number of years ago, an extremely pushy woman called us from San Francisco on the day of our anniversary and told us that she was preparing to cook a gourmet meal for us and expected us to arrive at her home by 6 that evening. We told her that we were sorry, but that this was our wedding anniversary.

We had already made reservations, and it would have to be some other time. She said, "I am sorry that you'll have to cancel all your other plans, because I have purchased all the ingredients to cook a $2,500 meal for you both tonight, and you need to be here. No excuses." We came to find out that we had to come on that night because her unbelieving husband would be out of town on a business trip. He would not have approved of us, as pastors, being in his home.

After some "intense fellowship" with my wife, we arrived at their home and found it almost impossible to pass through the halls of the house. She had three complete sets of brand new furniture that she told us she planned to regularly swap out in order to keep variety. When we sat down to the rather ordinary meal, which I would have given a score of 6 out of 10, and would have thought we were being robbed if we paid over $25 including tax and tip, she began sharing her long list of boring, rather weird dreams and even suggested she and I would be traveling together in the future in ministry overseas. I told her that this would only be possible if she were to get approval from my wife, which I knew would be totally out of the question. When we finally got an opportunity to come up for air and leave, we both agreed that we would never allow any meal at any price, even $2,500, to disrupt our anniversary plans again.

Humor in Ministry
A TEN-DOLLAR TV TRADE-IN

One day I came across an intriguing offer while scouting through the advertisement section of our local newspaper. I had been raised by very frugal grandparents who lost all of their considerable wealth during the depression of the 1930s, and they were barely getting by with my mother, who was a Canadian Air-Force WWII widow. This, out of necessity, had taught me to be a thrifty bargain hunter, pinching every last penny. My wife and I, who had just moved back from the U.S. to Canada and had just gotten new jobs, were desirous of purchasing our first television set. We, of course, were searching for the most reasonable rock-bottom price.

The ad stated that the appliance and electronic store would give a $50 rebate on a trade-in to those purchasing a new TV. I got a clever idea to scrummage through some old second and even third-hand stores, to look for a trade-in. I finally found a nice looking, old TV set that had a huge cabinet with a tiny screen for $10. The proprietor of the store assisted me in getting it into my 1951 Chevy and tying it down the best we could, despite the fact that it was huge, clumsy and on wheels.

The route back to our apartment required that I climb a very steep hill. As I was driving up the hill, I noticed in my rearview mirror that the TV had gotten loose and was rapidly rolling down the hill. Vehicles were swerving back and forth across the street in order to dodge this out-of-control, oncoming object. I stopped my car and began running full speed down the hill chasing my precious $10 merchandise. I prayed that God would somehow grant me mercy so that the TV didn't hit a car or pedestrian. When I finally got the TV back into the trunk of the car, I drove it back to the apartment where I needed to store it for the next couple of days until I could get the rest of the money to purchase the new TV.

Our apartment was on the third floor and there was no elevator. It was a horrendous struggle to get the TV up the stairs, and after having it fall back on me several times, I finally made it. I plugged it in; immediately dark grey smoke poured out of the set, and a loud popping noise followed, which blew out one of those old-time fuses. A few days later I got a friend to assist me in getting this potential trade-in to the appliance and electronics store to hopefully make the transaction for the new TV offered in the advertisement.

When we got there and I told the salesman that it did not work, he said I should have read the fine print of the advertisement that apparently stated that the $50 trade-in was for good working TVs only. He then indicated that the store had stopped taking any more trade-ins, as it was too much of a hassle. He also said that they had just lowered the price on new TVs by $50 to accommodate that change, and I would not need to trade-in my TV, anyway. The salesman suggested that we put the old antiquated non-operable TV out behind the store and the junkmen would come along and pick it up soon.

LESSON LEARNED: Make it a practice to always read the fine print before you complicate your life by trying to save a few extra dollars, which you were never entitled to in the first place.

CHAPTER 5

Patrick's Miracle Story

OSES VEGH AND I RETURNED ON FEBRUARY 20, 1973 from an intense 41-day missions trip around the world, having ministered in 17 different nations. We experienced God's supernatural manifest presence opening up numerous exciting doors, which were not even on our travel itinerary. Nevertheless, it was high time that we returned home to the realities and responsibilities of everyday living. Moses had a wife and six children and a large church, and they desperately needed him to return. And as for me, besides being a pastor, I was preparing to be the father of our first child, and my wife of seven years was seven months pregnant. We were looking forward with great anticipation to this life-changing event, which the doctor indicated was right on schedule and was expected to be a normal, uneventful birth. Instead it turned out to be one of the greatest crises of our lives, up until that time. My wife experienced 40 hours of hard, painful labor, resulting in having to have a C-section due to a severe case of toxemia. When I left the hospital after midnight on the seventh of April, the doctor said the baby was normal and doing extremely well.

This, of course, brought a major sigh of relief. He told me that it was time to go home and rest, and he would see me later. At 4 a.m. I was abruptly wakened by a startling phone call from the doctor stating that I needed to get down to the hospital immediately to sign release papers to have the baby moved by ambulance to Children's Hospital as Patrick was not doing well.

Baby Patrick was immediately placed in an ICU ward in an incubator with full life support, which seemed so contrary to the first diagnosis we received just after he was born. Patrick was on 100 percent oxygen and was diagnosed with what was then called Hyaline Membrane Disease, which meant that his lungs were premature and deflated, and he could not breathe on his own. John F. Kennedy's son Patrick Kennedy had died of the same disease.

On the eleventh day of baby Patrick's life, the pediatrician called us in and stated that Patrick had a 1 in 40 chance of living and that, if he made it, he would more than likely have some physical defects due to being on 100 percent oxygen for such a long period of time. He also informed us that the medical insurance we had was inadequate, and we would not be able to afford 24/7 attendant care. There was also a shortage of machines, and the machine servicing Patrick could be given to someone with a better prognosis. The doctor strongly suggested that we consider pulling the plug.

A man in our church at that time offered to purchase a machine, if there was a shortage. We were extremely thankful; however, praise God that we never needed it. That day we received two confirmations that everything was going to be all right even though, in the natural, it looked pretty hopeless. First, my mother told me about a prophetic word that she had received when she was paralyzed after my father had been killed in a fiery air crash near the end of World War II. The word was that my mother was going to be raised up to preach a brand new message, and that the son in her womb was going to be raised up to be a prophet to the nations, and that out of his loins was going to come forth another son who would also become a prophet to the nations. Remember, this was before ultrasound. My mother stated that Patrick had received a prophetic word in 1945, 28 years before he was born. Like Jeremiah, who was called to be a prophet to the nations long before he was born, she said, quite emphatically that Patrick cannot die. This seemed almost untrue at that moment. Within a few hours, a second prophetic word came through Pastor David Schoch, who phoned me and said, "David, your son cannot die because he is going to live, and within 17 hours he is going to be breathing normally on his own." Up until that moment, Patrick had not breathed one moment without life support. True to the word of the Lord, within ten hours, we received word from the hospital that baby Patrick was breathing 50 percent on his own, and the numbers kept moving up until the sixteenth hour when doctors stated that they were able to turn off all the machines because Patrick was breathing normally on his own. A few days later we brought him to the church on Easter (Resurrection) Sunday and dedicated him.

In 1992, at 19 years of age, Patrick was with me at a leadership conference in the Philippines. A Bible college was having a graduation for 100 students, and they needed a speaker to come and deliver a commencement address. They then requested that each student be baptized and given a word of prophecy. I was glad that I was already committed at the conference so that Patrick could go and experience this kind of ministry opportunity. Up until this time he had only prophesied on a few occasions. That day the prophetic word that had been decreed upon him in 1945 came into full view. Patrick has been preaching and prophesying ever since in several nations on a number of continents, as well as in numerous states in the U.S.

As Patrick would say, in times of crisis, receiving a word from God is not optional.

CHAPTER 6

Ventura Beach Provision

THE HARDEST PART ABOUT PREACHING FOR ME WAS that I had to live it myself. And that is often a pretty challenging contradiction, particularly with your own family who knows you the best. They are not as impressed with your ecclesiastical titles and platform performance as they are with how you conduct the normal affairs of your life.

Money was a very scarce commodity while my two children were growing up, even though my wife was a bargain hunter, clipped coupons and shopped for the kids' clothes in second-hand stores. We lived pretty frugally. We never had anything extra with a $1,000 to $1,200 per month salary. This salary was for both me and my wife who worked part-time for the church.

Consequently, we could never afford to go on extended vacations unless I preached somewhere every night and received an honorarium, a hotel and perhaps a couple of meals. We would vacation all day and then arrive for the service just in time. I obviously had no time to prepare, so I would reuse old messages, featuring the same illustrations, and the same jokes. My children would sit in the back. They knew the sermons very well, and they would be mouthing them, which at times was very distracting to me.

My daughter, Melinda, would ask me if the stories I was telling were true or was I "just preaching." One day we were returning home from Southern California, and we were almost financially broke. We stopped at Ventura Beach off Highway 101 for a brief break. We had been praying that morning that God would work a miracle so that we would at least have enough money to buy gas to get home and maybe get a meal on the way. We stepped into the ocean in about a foot of water and found a wallet with $600 in it, which for me at that time was two weeks' salary. The wallet had no ID in it, and my kids thought that this was a tremendous miracle from God. They felt it was time to party, and no one would be any the wiser for it.

They were looking to see what I was going to do next, and believe me, it was very tempting to just do a victory dance and go on a spending spree. That very moment I felt God speak clearly to me that this was a set up. This was an opportunity of a lifetime to not only teach, but to demonstrate what honesty and integrity look like. So, we took the wallet to the local police department to turn it in. They were kind of shocked that we were doing this when we had technically no obligation to do so, but they did explain that usually people did come looking for lost wallets, although that had not happened yet.

No amount of money would have ever been worth keeping in comparison to the valuable lesson that the kids learned that day. By the way we had just barely enough money to get back home and were able to get a couple of meals on the way. It was an unforgettable experience.

CHAPTER 7

Melinda's Story

IN THE YEAR 2000, WHEN MELINDA WAS ABOUT FOUR months pregnant, a routine ultrasound revealed the heartbreaking news that the baby boy she was carrying had a serious condition called skeletal dysplasia, which causes dwarfism and deformities of the bone. The pregnancy was extremely difficult with many tears and ups and downs. But Javier and Melinda received supernatural peace as the Shiloh Church family, as well as people around the world, upheld them in a blanket of prayer.

During the entire pregnancy, the whole family stood together in faith, believing for a miracle. We were trusting that our lives were in His hands, knowing that His ways are higher than our ways. The Lord gave Javier and Melinda the name "Isaiah" for the baby because it means "God is our salvation and helper." They knew they had to trust fully in the Lord to be their refuge in this time of trouble.

Isaiah Samuel Ramos was born by C-section on July 19, 2000, weighing 6 lbs. 5 oz. He was a beautiful baby with a generous amount of dark hair. The doctors soon discovered that they had drastically misdiagnosed Isaiah's condition. Instead, he had a fatal disease called Osteogenesis Imperfecta Type 2, which means his bones were constantly breaking. They knew their time with their sweet baby would be brief. They enjoyed

38 precious hours singing to him, talking to him and holding him. He looked at them with such peace and love in his eyes. Isaiah went to be with the Lord on July 21, 2000, and is now resting in the arms of Jesus.

The funeral was a beautiful time with the presence of the Lord clearly there. Just as we were finishing the burial, a little child ran up to Melinda and told her, "Look! There's a rainbow!" She didn't quite believe him because it was a hot day with no rainclouds in sight. But as we looked up, we beheld a very vivid, large rainbow that seemed to have no beginning and no end. Another smaller rainbow was above it. It stayed until the end of the burial, and then faded gently into the sky. On the evening news, the rainbow was described as a phenomenon because it had not rained in weeks. We know, however, that it was God's reminder to us that, "He will never leave us or forsake us." He loves us with an everlasting love. Even many non-Christians called it some kind of "sign."

At the time of the rainbow, a member of Shiloh had a vision of Isaiah sitting in his Father God's arms in heaven, and they were looking down at all the people mourning at the funeral. God said, "Son, would you like to do something special for the people to comfort them?" Isaiah said, "Oh yes, I would, Father." Then the Father painted a stunning rainbow across the sky as a promise of His great love.

Since then, Javier and Melinda have seen His promises fulfilled in such awesome ways. There were moments when they just had to continue to trust in His perfect plan for their lives, like when Melinda miscarried, or when the doctors told them that there was a 50 percent risk of the disease reoccurring when she became pregnant again.

But contrary to the doctor's report, in the fall of 2001, a sophisticated ultrasound revealed a perfectly formed baby boy, swimming and kicking in her womb. The whole family felt blessed beyond comprehension. Yes, precious little Joshua was on the way. And my, he was active. Javier could feel and see him kick right through the stomach. Our joy was endless. Here was their "rainbow" baby on the way. Their neighbor summed it up well when she presented them with a skillfully made, hand-knit rainbow blanket, with the attached note, "Your pot of gold at the end of the rainbow."

Joshua was born in 2002, healthy and whole. What a gorgeous baby boy! But the enemy did not want to see this promise come to full fruition. When Joshua was almost four months old, after feeling a strong impression to check on him, Melinda found him not breathing while he was taking a nap. After respiration measures seemed inadequate, he was rushed to Children's Hospital to receive emergency care. At first the prognosis was not good, but the Lord intervened, and the baby became responsive.

He spent a week recovering in the hospital, all the while undergoing a battery of tests. The results were inconclusive. All the doctors could say was that his blood counts indicated that he had faced a life-threatening experience. They said that he likely had a "near miss" with SIDS (Sudden Infant Death Syndrome). He would have died had Melinda not found him in time. We know that it was the Holy Spirit prompting her to check on him. We serve a faithful God whose promises are solid and true. He's a God of healing and restoration.

Even though we knew God had spared him, not all of Joshua's challenges were over, yet. In addition to being oxygen-deprived, his little body was rapidly pumped with large amounts of medicines and antibiotics upon arrival at the hospital to help combat any illness he might be facing. This caused his immune system to be compromised, and he faced several bouts of croup, ear infections and other infections. The littlest virus could cause his temperature to soar to 105 degrees, which would in turn result in febrile seizures that racked his body. Other health issues arose, and he needed occupational and physical therapy. Braces were put on his legs, while speech therapists dealt with his speech impediments. His kidneys were carefully monitored for a year when he faced an autoimmune disease. But our family kept pressing in for healing. This was the boy that the Lord had promised. We wouldn't give up! And our God is a God of miracles. He is able to do exceedingly and abundantly above all we could ask or think. Today we give Him all the glory because Joshua is completely healed and healthy!

The Lord had another special rainbow blessing for the Ramos family. Prophetic words had been spoken over Javier and Melinda describing two children dancing around the house. They held fast to the promise while Melinda struggled to get pregnant again, and then miscarried two more times. In February 2006, a lively, outgoing Cristiana Faith joined the family and brought a lot of sunshine to our lives. She is creative, artistic and joyful. We give praise to the Lord for His goodness. God has truly turned our sorrow into laughter, our tears into joy and thanksgiving! He is faithful to heal the brokenhearted and binds up their wounds (Psalm 147:3)!

When I spoke at Isaiah's funeral, I shared that faith always gets rewarded. Even when we do not get our answers in one season, God is always faithful to ensure that the answer will come in the next season. This was powerfully demonstrated in the lives of the Ramos family with the birth of Joshua and Cristiana, even when the odds were totally against them.

CHAPTER 8

Gift of Friendship

PASTORS ARE OFTEN THE LONELIEST PEOPLE IN THE WORLD; they don't need to hire a life coach as much as they need a true friend who will remain loyal and committed to them in all seasons. There is a difference between friendship and fellowship. Pastors enjoy and regularly engage in church fellowship. Fellowship means partaking in the activities, deeds and values of the gathered.

Friendship is having a genuine interest in a person and caring very deeply for them. Jesus was a friend of sinners; He felt more comfortable with them than the synagogue crowd. There are people who will gather around you in your success, but who will abandon you if you are a failure. You find out who your true friends are when you get into trouble. A true brother is born for adversity. Moses Vegh was my true friend and brother, and I am eternally grateful for the gift of friendship we shared.

Moses Vegh was saved in his early teens, and called into ministry shortly after his conversion. He and his wife Betty married in 1953, in Windsor, Ontario, Canada. They were blessed with 6 children, 17 grandchildren and 8 great-grandchildren. Moses is recognized by many emerging leaders as a "father" with an apostolic mantle. Moses pioneered and planted churches for almost 60 years, including the founding of Hope

Temple in Findlay, Ohio, where he and Betty pastored for 27 years. Moses laid spiritual foundations and was instrumental in planting several outreach churches in that area. He helped launch the first National Worship Symposium in Findlay, Ohio, which grew into a worldwide model for teaching praise, worship and orchestral excellence. In January 1986 he began ministry through Ambassadors of Hope to the Nations, and was ordained under Shiloh Christian Fellowship. He and I traveled and ministered together to over 35 nations.

I met Moses in Monterey, Mexico in 1971 at a Bible college graduation of 200 students where I happened to be the principal speaker. I tried desperately to get out of going and had given the directors of the college several alternative names to contact, but they could not find a person to fill in for me. I had just been away ministering in Brazil and Peru and had only been home one week. I was still pretty worn out from that trip.

A few weeks before, the Lord had told Moses that soon he would receive a call to go to California where he had never been and that he was going to form some brand new affiliations, as he was just coming out of his denomination. Little did either of us know that this rather chance meeting would begin a lifelong friendship and ministry partnership that would last over 40 years.

Moses was 12 years older than me, and, although I was raised without a father, we became close brothers and confidants rather than becoming a father and son relationship. I believe it was much like a Jonathan and David friendship. It was not some kind of superficial ministerial relationship where you only stayed in contact with people as church business dictated, if you positioned yourself correctly. Rather, I am talking about a person who will be there in times of your success and will not abandon you in times of your failure. Moses was always there. Although Moses and I always lived hundreds or even thousands of miles apart, we remained in contact with one another almost weekly by phone, when we were not otherwise ministering together in over 35 nations, as well as in numerous states where we were privileged to experience many phenomenal Book of Acts type miracles (which I will mention elsewhere in this book).

Moses and his wife, Betty, were ordained under Shiloh Church in Oakland for over 25 years, so we obviously had a unique relationship. God knows who to put in your life in order to push you into your next level. You need to have both Timothys and Pauls in your life, both those who pour into you and those whom you pour into. This is not only necessary for your growth and development, but it will also hold you accountable.

Moses and I were different. I was kind of reserved and content to stay in the background and out of the limelight. Moses was a gregarious, outgoing, joyful person who always ended up in the front row in the reserved section, whether he was invited there or not! He acted as if he belonged there, and nobody seemed to know the difference because of the way he carried himself, as an elder statesman. Whenever I was present, he always made sure that I had a seat next to him in the section where all the celebrities sat. As for me, I did not particularly care to meet them. If it had not been for our relationship, I would have probably stayed in my shell forever. So, God knows what or whom you need to push you forward and enlarge your capacity to fit into situations that you would not otherwise experience.

In the late fall of 2013, Moses, at the age of 80, was diagnosed with fourth stage stomach cancer. He passed away just a few weeks later. Moses must have had some premonition that he was going to be transitioning soon because in his book that was published just a short time before he passed on he wrote, "Today in a vision I am standing on Mount Nebo as Moses did ... and I am looking forward and outward and not backward."[2] My friend may have known his time on earth was short, but he

2. *The Chronicles of Moses: The Acts of an Apostolic Journey,* Moses Vegh, June 15, 2013.

was not planning to die anytime soon. We were scheduled to leave for Malaysia and Borneo in less than 30 days.

The Holy Spirit led me to bring his whole family together a couple of weeks before he died, including his children and grandchildren, so that he and Betty could lay hands on each of them. This was so that, just as the patriarch Jacob laid hands on his sons, Moses could proclaim their prophetic destiny and place his spiritual mantle upon them. Some family members thought I was rushing the process because Moses looked so well. It is vital to obey God when He prompts you to do something and not hesitate, because you could miss out on a once-in-a-lifetime opportunity. Moses on a number of occasions stated that his arrows were going to go further than he. This means that whatever we have passed on to the next generation, both spiritually and naturally, should produce more fruit than we were able to do in our generation. I believe that everyone in the room received a spiritual impartation that would carry them on into their future calling.

Most pastors I know do not need a paid life coach or a mentor or even an online leadership course as much as they need a true friend: someone they can be completely open, honest and vulnerable with. They need someone who will speak the truth in love without judging them, but at the same time will hold them accountable. This was the gift of friendship that God gave me for 40 years with Moses Vegh. I am eternally grateful for God sovereignly causing East and West to meet, and in turn changing my life forever.

Humor in Ministry
FINDLAY FUNERAL

On a cold, snowy day in Findlay, Ohio, while traveling in the car to go to lunch, our friends Pastor Moses and Betty Vegh remembered that they needed to stop by a funeral home to do a quick service. Feeling somewhat embarrassed, they apologized as they had to leave us in the car with the heater running. They hurriedly made their way to the chapel where the people had already been gathered for some time. Pastor Moses went up in his normal, eloquent manner to the podium and began officiating the funeral. When his wife noticed that the person in the open casket was a total stranger to them, she signaled to Moses to look over to the casket and view the unknown remains. When he finally did, he told the mourners that he was just there to start the service, and there would be another minister, no doubt coming along shortly to conclude the service.

A few minutes later, they both came out the door, laughing uncontrollably, causing my wife and me to wonder what kind of a funeral service they had attended. When they got in the car, they explained that this was the wrong funeral home, and the person in the casket was somebody they had never seen before. We then drove another 20 minutes across town to another mortuary where the mourners had been waiting for nearly an hour.

LESSON LEARNED: If you are ever called upon to officiate a funeral for someone, it would be best to check out the occupant in the casket prior to beginning the service.

CHAPTER 9

The John Garlington Story

OUR FAMILY, WHICH IS PRIMARILY MADE UP OF ministers, has always believed that the greatest privilege a true child of God can ever experience is to hear a *rhema* word from God.[3] Jesus made it abundantly clear that the way to distinguish between the sheep and the goats was based on whether they were receiving their guidance and direction from the voice of the Good Shepherd, or leaning entirely on their own human understanding.

In the Book of Amos, the prophet states that in the last days there will be a famine, not for bread or water, but for hearing or listening for the Word of God. There is more of the Word available today than there has ever been in history, but much of it is going over people's heads. They are often only absorbing the sound bites and have an inability to concentrate, so the meaning just passes them by.

The Bible indicates in James chapter 1 that any believer who fails to act upon the Word spoken is living in self-deception. We have a generation of Christians today whose desire is to be intellectually stimulated and entertained with "feel good"

---

3. In the New Testament, two Greek words are translated "word." Logos refers to the total inspired Word of God and to Jesus. *Rhema* refers to the spoken word, literally meaning "utterance." Luke 1:38; 3:2; 5:5 and Acts 11:16 contain the word *rhema*.

sermons but no convicting message. They want this feeling more than they want to be transformed and changed. We need to accept fully the fact that we are all a product of divine, sovereign election. God is the chooser, and we are the chosen. The Apostle Paul said, "I am what I am by the grace of God."[4] Therefore, my future destiny and calling is determined solely by the will of God and not the will of man. Paul fully embraced the fact that there was an appointed time or season for the fulfillment of every prophetic promise and, therefore, we have no need to strive to bring it to pass in our own energy. God is rarely in as big of a hurry as we are. Nothing happens by accident or coincidence. Often new ministries and prophetic callings are birthed out of extreme challenges and even tragedies such as the unusual crisis that suddenly thrust and catapulted my wife and me into positions as senior pastors at Shiloh Church.

In January of 1986, we were not in any way desiring the senior pastor positions, particularly because I had just lost a kidney about a month before and was still trying to regain my health. We did not want any additional responsibility. We had been serving and laboring alongside my mother, the late Dr. Violet Kiteley, as co-pastors for 16 and 1/2 years and ministered from the pulpit two Sundays out of the month. I had also been serving as the president of the corporation since 1970. We were perfectly content to remain in the co-pastor role for the rest of our ministry tenure.

However, God had other plans, which were very extreme in how they manifested. I received a phone call late on a Thursday night from John Garlington, a well-known, no-nonsense, proven prophet, stating that I needed to come to Portland, Oregon as soon as possible that night, and it was about 8 p.m. He told me he was leaving for a vacation/ministry trip with his wife at noon the next day, and it was imperative that I see him in person before he left Portland. He stated he had an urgent message he needed to give me before he and his wife flew out. I called around to all

---

4. 1 Corinthians 15:10.

the airlines and phoned him back telling him that it would be impossible to get a flight out that night for the short 600-mile trip north. I told him I booked a flight out first thing in the morning and would arrive at the Portland airport at 8 a.m. When I arrived, John was waiting for me curbside in his car.

After I got into the car and we exchanged brief greetings, he looked directly at me with his large introspective, piercing eyes and asked me when was I planning on obeying the Word of God? This was a rather challenging introduction; I wasn't sure at the time what he meant by that. We drove around Portland for about an hour as John Garlington showed me a number of homeless shelters, food ministries and other places where he, his wife and his church, Maranatha, were doing effective outreach work. These were a model for the whole region and state.

John then told me that he felt a strong impression that it was time for me to take over the reins and become the senior pastor of Shiloh. He stated that this transition needed to take place very soon, and he would come and present what he believed to be a prophetic mandate to my mother who had no idea whatsoever that I was in Portland having this discussion with him. John and his wife had a trusted, covenant relationship with my mother and Shiloh, and I felt comfortable with him being the one to break the news to her. He also wanted to talk to her about her future calling in expanding the ministry of the Shiloh Bible College, as well as more national and international travel.

Again, Marilyn and I were not seeking a promotion of any kind, particularly if it meant replacing my mother. We felt called to protect and serve her for the foreseeable future. So, this whole matter was really quite awkward and uncomfortable, to say the least. When I arrived home, I shared this with my wife. We made a solemn promise that we would not share this prophetic counsel with absolutely anyone, particularly my mother.

About a week later, we took a brief excursion to Lake Tahoe, a time of much-needed rest and relaxation. Everything was going extremely well until we received an emergency phone call stating that John and his wife, Yvonne, had been hit head-on by an 18-wheeler and were instantly killed in the State of Florida. At that moment, I began to reflect on the fact that John had been so insistent that I come up to Portland immediately before he was going to leave with his wife the next day at noon for a trip. At the time, it made absolutely no sense at all even though I went along with it. I couldn't help but wonder why the whole matter, which I was not all that enthused about, could not wait until he and his wife returned from their ministry vacation trip. The most perplexing question, however, was who was going to break the news of this prophetic mandate to my mother. Believe me, it was very tempting to put this whole proposition on hold and just mourn the loss of our friends, with whom we had traveled and ministered in presbytery on a number of occasions.

Later the next week, on an extremely stormy day, we went to the funeral in Portland at Maranatha Church. It was attended by bishops and pastors and dignitaries, including the governor of Oregon, the mayor of Portland and members of the state assembly as well as spiritual leaders from across the nation, whom John had imparted through his strong prophetic gift and holistic ministry. His uncanny, straightforward and accurate prophecies had set the course of many major ministries throughout the country and abroad. After this incredibly powerful, God-honoring home-going for John and his wife, I proceeded with my mother to look into the two caskets. With fear and trembling I attempted to relate to her the prophetic word John had given me concerning replacing her, wondering all the while how she was going to respond. My mother was a 100 percent, seriously committed, 24/7 minister who had never married after my father died. Her only interest in life was the Kingdom of God. To my amazement, her response was extremely positive. This was primarily because her basic philosophy in life was that hearing from God was not an option. She firmly believed that when God spoke, it was meant to be acted on immediately, without delay or hesitation.

I shared John's prophecy with her on a Friday, and she immediately responded that we would make the announcement at Shiloh in two days on Sunday. And from then on, the church would be entirely in my wife's and my hands, and my mother would follow my lead in whatever way I felt the Lord was taking the church. If you can imagine, there was no pomp and circumstance or celebration of any kind. There was no prior planning or Board of Directors meeting, or even congregational announcements or outside ministry to set us in to the senior pastor positions with prophecy and laying on of hands. My mother simply got up Sunday morning and very graciously related the word of God from the late John Garlington, and reiterated the unusual tragic circumstance, which had left us all with no other option than to abruptly make a leadership transition in this manner. She stated that, had John lived, he was planning to declare this message both to her and to the elders of the church. At that moment, she turned the church over to my wife and me and took her seat in the front row, ready to accept an expanded role in the Bible College and do more national and international travel. She was scheduled to preach that morning, so I had not prepared a message, but now, suddenly, it was in my hands. So, it was incumbent upon me to come up with something. This was a very unconventional manner to be set in as senior pastors, and it was a very stretching experience for our leaders and congregation as well as us.

This, of course, would have never transpired if there were not such a high degree of respect and regard for the prophetic *rhema* word of God that must be followed to the letter, regardless of the cost.

CHAPTER 10

Unusual Welcoming Committee

OUR FAMILY MOVED FROM BRITISH COLUMBIA, Canada to the asphalt jungles of the San Francisco-Oakland Bay Area during the height of the Civil Rights Movement, the Vietnam War and the hippie/flower children era. This was a major cultural shock to our whole family, to say the least. Canada had historically been a sanctuary for African-Americans with its underground railroad during the horrible days of slavery. It was also, at that time, becoming a haven for U.S. Vietnam draft dodgers. We soon realized that we had immigrated to the U.S. in the mid-60s with a high degree of ignorance and naiveté. Little did I know that a good dose of reality was going to be setting in really quickly.

I began working in a real estate title insurance company in downtown Oakland, and I discovered, after a short period of time, that there were still restrictive property laws in certain regions of the city where African-Americans were not permitted to purchase or even own a home. In some cases, they did not even allow African-Americans to drive through these restrictive neighborhoods, which, to me, was a total travesty. I was tempted to quit my job and go back to Canada. One day, I came out of our rented house and was horrified to find that the four wheels of my car had been removed, and the vehicle was sitting on the ground with the wheels stacked beside it.

A young African-American walked up to me and angrily asked me what I was doing in the neighborhood, to which I replied I did not know anything about the neighborhoods. I told him that I had just emigrated from Canada with my mother and elderly grandparents and we had moved into a home in this community because we found the rent affordable. He became instantly very apologetic and began giving me the history of the neighborhood where he had grown up with his family and told me that he worked in downtown Oakland. I asked him how he got to work, and he said that he rode on the city transit buses. I told him that I would make a deal with him. If he would assist in putting the wheels back on the car, I would drive him downtown to the company where he worked, which was just a block away from where I worked.

We became close friends and I had the privilege of praying with him to receive Jesus as his personal Savior. He started coming to our church and was very committed until he later moved to the East Coast. The last I heard he was on staff with a flourishing ministry.

LESSON LEARNED: Long-lasting friendships are not always birthed out of the most ideal situations, and God will take the worst that the enemy of our soul can dish out and totally turn it around for His own glory. God used my friend to be an unusual welcoming committee.

Humor in Ministry
WILD ANIMAL SOUNDS

One Sunday morning at a Las Vegas church, I preached a message from the Book of Joel, chapter 2, on the last days. After the service, an elderly gentleman came up to me. He appeared to be very upset. He stated emphatically that he did not believe that these were the last days and that I should not be promoting fear from the pulpit. I asked him how old he was and he replied that he was 77. Without giving this conversation any further thought, I said, "Sir with all due respect, whether you agree or not, these are your last days."

That evening we had a long service in which I prayed and gave prophetic words of direction to almost everyone in the building, which was about 200. When I finally got back to my hotel room, I was totally exhausted and ready to retire to bed immediately. In the middle of the night, I thought I was experiencing a full on, last days, apocalyptic dream, complete with loud roaring, vicious, wild animals that were getting ready to attack me. I was so startled that I literally jumped out of bed, and I began anxiously trying to shake myself out of this frightening dream, which had, by then, accelerated into a full-blown nightmare.

When I finally woke up, got dressed and went outside on the balcony, I discovered that the roar of the vicious animals was continuing with even greater intensity. I went around to the back of the hotel and discovered several animal cages containing live lions and tigers lined up at the back of the driveway next to the hotel. I went into the lobby, and hotel security informed me that these exotic animals were used in the circus segment of one of the nightly shows at the hotel. He then asked me how many tickets I would like to buy for that night's show, which he claimed was nearly sold out. My first response was, why would I ever want to purchase tickets for this show when I already had a front row seat in my dream, complete with all the exotic wild animal sounds. People frequently ask me to interpret their dreams and from time to time the Lord gives me a word of knowledge, but I haven't got a clue to the significance of this dream, particularly as it relates to the last days. All I know for sure is: that was the last day I will ever stay in that hotel.

PART II
Pastoral Life

There is perhaps no calling in life quite as challenging and demanding as the life of a pastor who is truly called of God. Imagine being held accountable by God for the souls of those who have voluntarily chosen to be under your watch. That is a tall order indeed. During his third-year pastorate, the Apostle Paul reminded the church at Ephesus that he had literally been with them in all seasons, in times of sorrow and times of joy. My sincere desire is that the readers will commit themselves afresh to fully support, speak uplifting words of encouragement to and earnestly pray for their pastors. This may well be one of the toughest jobs on planet earth.

CHAPTER 11

A Baptism Miracle

THERE ARE ONLY TWO INCIDENTS IN THE NEW Testament where Jesus referred to someone as having great faith. In both of these unique situations, the individuals were not from the House of Israel and did not have a right to their covenant blessings.

The first was a Roman centurion. In the account found in Luke 7:1-4, he felt totally unworthy and sent the elders of the city to plead with Jesus to send a word of healing to his servant, who was desperately ill and on the verge of death. He believed the words of healing from Jesus's mouth were an enforceable imperial order, fully backed up by the authority of the heavens. Just as his words as a Roman centurion were backed up by Caesar and Rome, he believed if he could just get Jesus to speak the word only, his servant would be healed without Jesus ever having to come to his house.

The second was a mother, who, in Matthew 15:21-28, came to Jesus on behalf of her daughter who was severely demonized. This lady refused to be denied or offended or put off by anything which could have been interpreted as a negative or even racist response from Jesus. It was her persistent fight and intercessory prayer of importunity that caused Jesus to say directly to her, "Woman, great is your faith, let it be unto you as you have requested." Both of these incidents were vivid examples of individuals who came on behalf of somebody else and refused to give up prematurely. Often the most difficult season is right before the breakthrough. The question becomes, can you hang in long enough to obtain the desired results?

In the spring of 1968, we were just in the beginning stages of our pastorate in Surrey, British Columbia; Marilyn and I were in our early 20s. One day we got a call from a lady who seemed extremely distraught. She stated that she was not able to get any spiritual ministry for her aging father who was terminally ill in a medical care center. She told us she lived in a city about 45 miles from where we were located. She claimed she had called every church in the phonebook, of all denominations, between where she lived and where we were located, requesting that a minister come and pray for her father because he needed healing. But, she said, no one would come. Some said they would only come with the understanding that they were doing so to give her father his last rites.

She stated that even though they were Roman Catholics, they refused to accept that kind of prayer of finality. She believed that his life was not over yet, and God had more for him to do. I told her we were willing to come immediately, if she so desired, to which she replied, "No, I'm going to bring him to you because I believe he should be baptized with full immersion as Jesus did." So, I, being young and full of faith, optimistically stated without any reservations or counting the cost, "We take them in all conditions." We arranged for him to come at 11 a.m. the next day; then, after I hung up the phone, I began to wonder what I had gotten myself into. We started preparing the baptistery for the service and discovered the water line to the baptismal tank had been broken and the immersion heater was inoperable. So, we began bringing up cold water from the church basement in garbage cans in order to fill the baptistery in hopes that it would get warmer overnight.

Around 11 a.m. the elderly man and his daughter arrived in an ambulance. He was on a gurney with a number of monitors and apparatus hooked up to him, and was extremely weak and frail. When I saw him, I took his daughter aside and said, "Don't you think we should just sprinkle a little water on him and pray a healing prayer and get him back as soon as possible to the medical center?" Somehow the elderly gentleman overheard us and yelled out, "Absolutely not! I have already been sprinkled at the Catholic church, and now I want a full immersion. That is the only reason we came here today."

We did not have the nerve to tell him the water was ice-cold. The paramedics started to get very frustrated. They said they wanted nothing to do with this, and that, in their estimation, he would die if put in the water. Nevertheless, the daughter and the father both agreed that they would be willing to take full responsibility for what happened. So, with fear and trembling, I, along with one of the brothers from the church who happened to be a former hospital orderly, proceeded to take off the medical apparatus. We wheeled the gurney forward to the front of the church and then proceeded to lift it up onto the stage. The only way we could get him to the baptismal tank due to his condition was to carry him up the choir stairs then over the rails of the tank. The orderly got into the water and I held onto the frail man as tight as I could, considering he was completely dead weight. We unfortunately burnt his foot in the baptismal spotlight, to which he let out a blood-curdling yell. We said a brief prayer, placed him down on the top of the water and were barely able to get his back wet when he yelled out again saying, "You didn't put me all the way down!" Immediately we complied, but just hoped and prayed that God would give us the supernatural strength to get him back up, out of the tank and onto the gurney again. The daughter began thanking us profusely and seemed very grateful and relieved that her father was finally baptized by immersion. He was by then soaking wet and shivering like a leaf having been immersed in ice-cold water. Finally, the paramedics got him hooked up again and back into the ambulance. They turned on the flashing red lights, and headed back to the medical center 45 miles away.

Marilyn and I were greatly relieved that the whole ordeal was over; however, I was fully expecting to hear from the legal authorities or be arrested by the police. In our minds, that could have been the end of our pastoral ministry, which we had begun only six months before. By the end of the next week, however, I got a call from the daughter, rejoicing on the other end of the phone, and stating that her father had been completely healed in the waters of baptism and would be going home from the medical center the next day. Marilyn and I stated that this could have never transpired had it not been for the great faith and persistence of the daughter and the father who refused to give up and throw in the towel prematurely, despite the odds. They took a risk, and God honored their faith. This, along with our willingness to participate in the situation, though it was extremely challenging and uncomfortable at the time. I don't recommend that anyone attempt to do this unless they have actually heard an audible voice from the Lord.

While writing this story, I began recalling another dramatic incident that took place approximately a decade ago at the county hospital in Oakland. On a Saturday afternoon, one of our pastors, Leora Overall, who happened to be part of the chaplain service at Highland Hospital, called me to go and pray for a man by the name of Harold. The doctors had told Harold's family that he was not expected to live much longer. When I got to the hospital, I found that Harold was likely braindead and some of his family was assembled with him in the intensive care unit. I went into the room and prayed a brief prayer, read an appropriate scripture, gave a word of comfort to the family, gave my condolences and politely excused myself, fully expecting that that would be the last time I saw Harold. The next morning I received a phone call from the hospital, fully expecting them to inform me that he had passed. Instead they said, "We have renamed Harold. He's now called

Lazarus, and he's walking up and down the hospital corridor, and it was an absolute miracle." His wife came to church the next week to publicly confirm the miracle and to thank us for our prayers. I began to realize afresh how little we, personally, have to do with healing.

On some occasions, I have prayed my very best prayer and God in His sovereign foreknowledge has seen fit to take that person into His eternal presence. On other occasions, I have prayed what I considered a much more subdued, weak, anemic prayer, and the results were very positive, and people lived. God doesn't often tell us in advance what the final outcome will be, or else we would quit praying, but God always honors our availability. We are to be a life-giving conduit who declares His promises, regardless of what feelings we have about the situation.

Humor in Ministry

A POTATO FARMER FINANCES A YOUNG MAN'S DESTINY

In 1986, my late mother, Dr. Violet Kiteley, who never believed in ever missing an opportunity, was asked to speak at a Bible study at the San Francisco Conservatory of Music. It was there that she met a young man by the name of Doug McClure, who was studying music and had been playing the cello since he was nine years old. His initial response to hearing her speak was that she was pretty clearly a radical believer. He wasn't sure at the time whether he wanted to be part of her church. However, a few weeks later he showed up at our church in Oakland on Sunday.

My mother gave Doug a prophecy: the Lord was going to send him to the kings of the world, to many nations, and he would play before them and many of them would come into the Kingdom of God. At that point, he thought that she must have been totally off base and that this was something that could not possibly ever take place. Nevertheless, he was filled with the Spirit and began attending Bible college.

One day Doug made an appointment to speak with me. This poor college student was barely squeaking by and he drove to my office in an old, beat-up car with bald tires. Then he presented an exceptionally unusual request. He had found an old cello dated from the 1700s, worth about $200,000, at a music store in San Francisco, and he wanted to purchase it. I asked him how he ever expected to pay for the cello knowing that he probably did not have more than $20 in his wallet at the time. He told me about a multi-billionaire potato farmer in Boise, Idaho, who made his fortune by selling his potatoes to the McDonald's chain to make french fries. Doug said that, although he had never personally met him, he had heard about him all of his life, as he was raised in the same region. He then asked me if I would be willing to write a letter to this potato farmer, who he was sure was not a Christian, requesting that he purchase the cello for Doug. He wanted me to state that he would use it regularly to hold music concerts and Christian conferences.

I thought to myself that this kind of out of the blue, cold-calling was going to be a colossal waste of time. However, in the back of my mind, I could not help but admire the young man's faith. Who knows what could happen; it was at least worth giving it a try. I sat down and wrote a rather generic letter asking the billionaire if he would consider, in the interest of the arts, financing a young, highly skilled professional musician's dream. I told him that he would play this rare cello of renowned origin in many prestigious venues (none of which were scheduled at the time). I enclosed all of Doug's contact information, prayed over the letter and sent it off. I wasn't sure what results we could expect from this stab in the dark, random money solicitation.

A few days later, this extremely wealthy man, who no doubt had a large staff, personally called Doug. His initial response seemed to be extremely negative; it almost appeared as if the door was being slammed shut in his face. The billionaire then asked Doug, "Who are you anyway? Why are you calling me? I don't fund any musical projects. That is not my field."

Mild-mannered Doug was able to patiently allow this man to rant on until he released all of his negativism. He finally, as Doug would tell it, came to a sudden halt and began to turn the conversation in the opposite direction. The billionaire finally said, "Tell me where this cello is." He added, "I will have my staff arrange for you to bring it up here from San Francisco for a few days so that I can see it and hear you play it before I make any further commitments." Doug then told the billionaire that he did not have any money for an airline ticket, and they would have to purchase a ticket. He then told the man that he would need two tickets so that he could place the cello in a seat. When Doug went to visit him in Idaho, he began playing the cello, and the man's initial reaction was that he did not like cello music, so he asked Doug to stop playing because it hurt his ears. With that, Doug resorted to playing the cello like a fiddle and played some old western dance songs like "Turkey in the Straw." The old gentleman began dancing around the room and said, "Doug, you are good, son." From that moment on the deal was sealed and set in motion, and this billionaire purchased this old cello.

The prophecy that Pastor Violet gave Doug that he would play before kings was confirmed as he played before King Juan Carlos of Spain, King Abdullah of Jordan, former President Jimmy Carter, Pope John Paul II and at a celebration at the Vatican in St. Peter's Square before 300,000 people. Doug has also played before the United Nations, and the list goes on.[5] Who knows whom God is going to choose to use to finance your future prophetic destiny? It might be a potato farmer you have never met.

---

5. More information on Doug McClure's ministry can be obtained by contacting him at: dougmcclure7@yahoo.com.

CHAPTER 12

IHOP Fire

PERHAPS ONE OF THE GREATEST WEAKNESSES OF THE current Western Church is that many of its adherents have little or no confidence in their own prayers. Hebrews 4:2 states that the nation of Israel did not receive any profit from the Word spoken to them because it was not mixed with faith.

We are constantly hearing ministers declaring from their pulpits and television programs that what we need is more prayer to change the landscape of America and the world. I agree wholeheartedly as long as it is the right kind of prayer. Unfortunately, a lot of so-called prayer is nothing more than a hollow religious cultural ritual. It is like clouds with no water. And even though it may be well meant, there is no sense of expectation or anticipation of anything actually changing. It often gets stuck in the rafters. Prayer that is laced with doubt and unbelief is void of any demonstration of the power of God to heal the sick, deliver the oppressed or deal with emergencies because it is not mixed with faith. There is a vast difference between being led by the Spirit of God and being driven by circumstance.

One night after a phenomenal faith-building service in our church in Canada, Paul, a lifelong friend, and I agreed in prayer that God would give us an opportunity to put the Word that had been spoken that night into action. We had absolutely no idea of the adventure God had in store for us that evening. Paul had a habit of going out after church to 24-hour restaurants and sitting up most of the night drinking coffee. His primary purpose was to witness to anybody and everybody who came through the doors and was willing to listen.

I began hearing of some of the miracle conversions, deliverances and even healings that were taking place in these settings, so I decided to go and witness these testimonies first-hand, particularly because some of these individuals were beginning to attend our church. While driving past an IHOP restaurant en route to Paul's favorite "salvation fishing hole," we noticed that the kitchen was totally engulfed in flames, and smoke was filling the entire premises. The parking lot of the restaurant was empty, and it did not appear that there were any customers left on the property. Nevertheless, we strongly sensed the urgency of the Holy Spirit to risk going inside the restaurant.

We had absolutely no knowledge of what we were going to encounter when we got inside. Being young and fearless, we barged into the IHOP and began attempting to battle the smoke and the flames by crawling on the floor without any fire gear. We accidentally stumbled onto the cook who was lying unconscious on the kitchen floor, completely overcome with smoke. We quickly dragged him outside and called 911. We then began to administer CPR as we prayed fervently that God would spare his life. After a considerable amount of time, the cook started coming to. We considered this whole ordeal to be divinely orchestrated, because within a short period of time the whole building became engulfed in flames. The building had to be rebuilt after having to close for a long period of time.

When the cook finally came to, we told him how God must have really loved him and still had a strong purpose yet for his life. We said that we had prayed after our church service that night that God would send us on a special mission even though we obviously had no idea we would be involved in saving a person's life at an IHOP, and that we had planned on going to another restaurant. The cook accepted Jesus and later started attending our church when his shifts permitted. We also had the opportunity to pray for the firemen, police and first responders as we stayed there for several hours filling out reports related to the fire and the lifesaving rescue. They told us over and over again that we were heroes, and they were going to write the story up in the local newspaper, as well as nominate us for a reward for bravery and lifesaving, which at the time was of little interest to us.

LESSON LEARNED: Don't ask God to use you in any way He sees fit, unless you are willing to walk through all of the doors marked opportunity, some of which may be more desirable than others. This is what it means to be led by the Spirit of God through heartfelt prayer rather than be driven by circumstances.

CHAPTER 13

Restoring Fallen Ministry

I T WAS JUST 65 YEARS AFTER JESUS'S DEATH, BURIAL, resurrection and ascension, when the church of Ephesus received a message directly from the Lord Jesus.[6] It was from this great church that all of Asia Minor heard the gospel in the space of just two and half years, without the aid of modern technology. The economic transformation was so intense that the idol-making business in the temple of Diana and Artemis, which was the main industry of the region, went bankrupt. A huge bonfire was held and all the books on curious magic and the occult, which affected the entire culture, were burned. Now, like a lot of subsequent movements, which were noted for having a supernatural beginning, people did, over time, cool off and become indifferent. They had lost the power, presence and passion for the loving, intimate relationship that they once possessed with the Lord. They had, unfortunately, outgrown His counsel and were now leaning totally on their own understanding. They had become more concerned in their own status, image and notoriety than they were in actually extending the Kingdom of God.

The church of Ephesus had grown to 25,000 members and was the parent church for other churches, but the Lord Jesus said emphatically, "But I have this against you, that you have left

---

6. Revelation 2:1-7.

your first love."[7] This was not so much a word of condemnation or judgment as it was a word of disappointment and rejection. They had left their first love; the church of Ephesus had allowed their passionate love for Jesus to wane and had lost the initial spontaneity and fervor that they once had in their relationship with the Lord. Their ardent zeal was replaced by orthodox routine, complacency and apathy. God wanted the Ephesian church's attention afresh, and He desired to recreate and restore in them the fire of love that they initially experienced.

When you leave your first love, the protocols and even principles become more important than personal relationships. A loveless, religious, dutiful, works-based tradition takes precedence over relationship. It is God's desire to fan the flame of our love so that we do not end up becoming stagnant and having a lamp without any oil.[8] Jesus was saying, in effect, that He desired above all else that their former first love relationship would be restored, where He is no longer just considered Lord of the church, but also the lover of the church.

This leads me to recall a life-changing incident that occurred a number of years ago. One day I received a rather out of the blue, random call from a renowned minister who wishes to remain anonymous. He was inquiring whether I might possibly fit him into my busy schedule if he was to fly out and see me at the beginning of the next week. I agreed and cleared my calendar so I could give him my undivided attention. He had been in pastoral ministry, and traveled nationally and internationally, leaving a lasting impact wherever he'd gone. He had a reputation of being a highly successful pastor and had built some strong New Testament churches that had powerfully affected their communities and the entire regions where they were located. It is highly unusual for a minister of this caliber to ever go anyplace where they were not invited to be a keynote speaker at a major conference. After we met and engaged

---

7. Revelation 2:4.

8. Matthew 25:1 – 13.

in the normal ministerial chit chat concerning the who's who and the what's new in the religious scene, he started discussing why he had flown across the country to meet with me.

He began by saying how grateful he was that I was willing to take this time with him. There were very few places he knew where he could go as a broken shepherd to find help. He felt he could confide in me, and if he laid out his heart in an honest manner, it would not be blasted all over the nation. He said that he had perfect confidence after receiving a number of confirmations both from the Lord and other spiritual leaders that his secret would be safe and that he could expect to be taken through a process of restoration without being judged or condemned.

His story was how, for years in his early beginnings he had a strong prayer and devotional life, and each morning he'd developed the habit of listening to the Lord as He awakened his ear. He expected each day to receive fresh manna, which would guide all of his major ministerial decisions. He made it a practice to never go into the pulpit without a strong sense that God had given him a relevant timely *rhema* word for the congregation, which would not only bring refreshment to them but would restore his soul as well. He stated, however, as time went on, he began to rely more and more on his charismatic personality, gifting and ability to persuade the crowd; he began to function entirely on ministerial autopilot. He knew that his wife and family as well as the church leaders close to him were beginning to become very concerned about the fact that he was spending less and less time at the church. He'd been skipping out on staff meetings and making excuses for missing services even during major conferences. They had tried to tell him that he seemed to be growing more and more distant. He was restless and became annoyed at anyone who attempted to question his whereabouts. To make matters worse, the church was experiencing a "Gideon's revival," meaning more people were leaving fellowship than coming in, and this was very disheartening to him. He had forgotten the fact that the members of the congregation are the sheep of the Lord's pasture and that they were never his in the first place. He said he had tried to be an all season's pastor, and he had burnt the candle at both ends trying to serve these people. He felt that their lack of loyalty and faithfulness had been one of the major reasons that sent him into this tailspin.

Fortunately, he recognized that he had a wife who gave him space even though he knew that she was terribly upset, and she stated that she was having to see a counselor a couple of times a week just to maintain her sanity. We talked about the fact that fortunately, he'd never gone as far as to engage in extramarital affairs despite having thought about it and been given opportunity on several occasions. He made the statement that, "Obviously, God must still have some restraints on me. I know my wife is fasting and praying, and even though I'm at the lowest point that I have ever been in my life, I still have enough of the fear of God in me to keep me from totally going over the brink."

Listening to him in-depth, I heard him say that the past month, after 25 years of full-time ministry, he decided to take a year off for sabbatical. This was an attempt to get back to where he should be. "Right now, I have very little faith that it will happen because I am totally dry and barren and extremely depressed. I'm rarely able to get more than a few hours of sleep at night no matter the medication I take." He was like a man wandering in the desert and, although he should know better, he felt as if God had completely forgotten him. Feeling overwhelmed with cynicism caused him to be distrusting of everyone, and resentful of the fact that many of his so-called pastor friends across the nation and even his local ministerial team had not been reaching out to him. There was what he described as a sense of total aloneness, isolation and abandonment.

After many hours of spewing out all his complaints, he finally said, "Thank you for listening. I am sorry it was so long and drawn-out but as you can see I am totally desperate." We began to discuss the fact that the scriptures are made up of a lot of flawed people who were revived and rehabilitated and restored. We talked about the fact that there are no instant blowouts in ministry, only slow leaks and how the sheep do not wander away from the flock overnight. Their departure is usually one bite at a time. So consequently, when a person enters the failure zone, it is never the result of a momentary decision. However, the process of return can be greatly accelerated if we're willing to totally release all the blame and shame that has caused us so much pain and disappointment. I discussed with him the story of the prodigal and how the father viewed him from afar and ran toward him and kissed his neck and totally restored him. He was also given family emblems that proved his sonship. He began sobbing uncontrollably, and I had the privilege of praying for this man and simply requesting that God would somehow supernaturally touch his heart, his mind, his will and his emotions and make him soft and pliable once again. We prayed together that the Lord would restore his joy and that he would no longer be just functioning out of a sense of duty and tradition.

We agreed together that the first love relationship with the Lord that he once experienced would begin to flood his soul, even to a greater degree than he had ever known in the past. After a long-extended time of his completely opening himself up in a very vulnerable manner, he then began repenting of all the animosity that he had built up toward other people and even the Lord. We did not start to experience any real breakthrough until he began to recite a long list of individuals he felt had misused and abused him. He continued crying out to God and requesting that He wash him with His blood and cleanse his mind of all the contamination he had allowed to bring him to this point of demise. At this point he was totally exhausted and went back to his hotel to catch up on some rest. He called me later that evening and said that for the first time in months he had slept like a baby. He felt like he was newly saved and baptized in the Holy Spirit, and there was a renewed joy and peace and sense of hope that had evaded him for such a long time.

His major question at that point was whether or not he could ever be restored back to ministry again as he did not believe he

I DIDN'T MEAN TO CAUSE TROUBLE

was worthy. I reminded him of Peter who had failed openly, and Jesus, right in front of the rest of the disciples, re-commissioned him back to ministry. Jesus reordained him as a shepherd and told him to "Go and feed my sheep and minister to my lambs." After we spent a couple days together, he returned home. A couple months later he called and stated that he had been restored back to his pastorate. He was extremely grateful for the Lord's grace in giving him another opportunity to minister. He stated that he knew that he could never again allow himself to get into a place where he ignored the early warning signs. The call to the New Testament Church is to bring health, wholeness and rehabilitation in the spirit of meekness and humility that embodies the heart of our founder, Jesus, whose desire is always to restore fallen leaders.

Humor in Ministry
PUNCHED IN THE MOUTH

One Wednesday night I was teaching on spiritual warfare when a shirtless, barefooted man who appeared to be drunk or on drugs came through the doors of the church and started making his way down the aisle toward the front.

I made the mistake of going up the aisle to meet him and asked him if I could help him. His reply was, "Yes, you better believe you can!" and he punched me in the mouth, bloodying my lip and loosening a tooth. By that time, our men were on him, and one of them took off his own belt and soon had the man hog-tied and face down on the ground. In the meantime, I was attempting to calm the congregation down so there would not be a riot. I told the church that they needed to pray for this man as he probably had a lot more problems than we could ever know and a little blood on my mouth would heal but this man's soul needed healing. At this moment, I heard one of the deacons, who had his knee in the man's back saying, "These people are all Pentecostal, and they take care of your soul, but I am still Baptist and I am here to take care of your flesh."

They finally dragged him out, with the belt still tied around his hands, to the foyer. A policeman arrived, who happened to be a Catholic, and said, "How dare you hit the Father?" Our prisoner would have seriously hurt the police officer had we not calmed him down. Later on, the ushers apologized profusely to me, saying, "We're so sorry! We thought this guy was a part of your message; otherwise we'd never have let him in."

I then said, "One thing I want you to remember for the next time: if we are doing a play, and I am in the front preaching, it won't be me taking the hit because, in that case, I will always use a double."

Humor in Ministry
THE DISABLED HEARSE

According to Ecclesiastes 7:14, God designed life to be a strange mixture of adversity and prosperity, and He has set one against the other to bring a proper balance in life. However, it will take an eternity to reveal why some people have seemingly had more than their share of adversity from the cradle to the grave. Such was the life of a dear elderly saint in our church who was a long-term faithful member, and volunteered in any position where she could lend a needed hand.

When she finally passed on to her reward, our sincere desire was to make her home-going service and subsequent burial a memorable experience that would be free of adversity. Unfortunately, the mortuary elected to use an old 1959 Cadillac hearse to transport her body. This hearse had seen better days and should have been put off the road at least a decade or more before. My mother, Pastor Violet, and I, as the officiating pastors at the funeral, mistakenly decided to ride in this old relic with the stoic driver, who was totally expressionless.

We felt we were making the last trip in the hearse before it was being retired to the barn. It was an unusually cold, wet, rainy day in the San Francisco Bay Area, with high winds that, according to the weather report, were not about to let up.

The route to the cemetery required that, after traveling north for five miles, we make a sharp right turn in order to exit to the next freeway. At that moment the front right wheel of the hearse suddenly came off, and the vehicle slammed into the side of a high wall, causing the casket to shift from one side of the car to the other.

To make matters worse, we discovered that the bald old spare was flat, and it was unlikely that it would hold any air, anyway. The driver radioed the mortuary for assistance. The next minute, we were out on the freeway turnoff, attempting to direct traffic in our formal pastoral attire without any overcoats. We looked like drenched rabbits. Finally, after 20 minutes that seemed like an eternity, a beat-up, old, white, dirty panel van, which they used to carry flowers in, arrived, and we began carrying the casket on the roadway from one vehicle to another.

All the while, the impatient people in the waiting cars that were, by that time, backed up at least a mile, were shaking their fists, honking their horns and making obscene gestures toward us. They were, no doubt, thinking that we were making a trailer for an upcoming movie.

When we finally got back on the road, I could almost hear our departed sister speaking down to me directly from heaven, saying, "Dear Pastor, I am sorry to be such a bother again, but if you can just get me to the cemetery in one piece, I promise you that this is the last request that I will ever make."

LESSON LEARNED: Make sure to mention in your will, if you are desirous of having a traditional funeral, that whoever makes the arrangements should check out the hearse to see whether it is roadworthy and has a good set of tires to make your final trip on your earthly journey.

CHAPTER 14

Giver and Not a Taker

URING THE EARLY '80S A WOMAN CAME FROM San Francisco to our church as a pauper. Boldly she would ask anyone for a ride to church and to the doctors and to go shopping. She never offered to pay a cent for gas nor appeared to be all that thankful. She would walk several blocks from her house to a poorer neighborhood in order to be picked up so that no one would find out where she lived. Every Sunday, she would collect all the leftovers at the church as well as empty out the refrigerator. Often, she would go up to people as they were eating and ask them to give her anything that they were not able to finish.

This lady would apply for every scholarship that was available at the Bible college, and would request assistance available to pay for conferences when fees were required. She picked up all the old cans in the kitchen to redeem. She would often ask people to assist her in paying for her phone or utility bills. Her favorite verse was found in Matthew 25, which she quoted regularly, "When you have done it unto the least of these you have actually done it unto Jesus himself."

She applied for every assistance plan available and would write letters asking people to sponsor her if the church seniors were going on an outing. One might say that she must have been mentally incapacitated, but, to the contrary, she was very brilliant and would earn straight A's in the Bible college, always expecting to receive all degrees without paying any fees. Everything she did was deliberate, intentional and premeditated. My mother and I both agreed as compassionate pastors to be the executors of her trust at the time of her death. We had absolutely no idea what assets she possessed. One day we were handed a notarized letter stating that we were the executors, and that if we needed to find out anything, we could find it in the top drawer of her bedroom dresser. She also provided the address of her home, which we had never visited.

We never knew very much about her, as she was a very private person; all we knew was that she was a widow and had faithfully attended our church for over ten years and appeared to be a very needy person. One day we began to realize that we had missed her for a few weeks, so we drove over to her home in San Francisco to check up on her. When we inquired of the neighbors, they informed us that they also had not seen her in a few weeks. They were concerned about her and were glad that we had come as they were preparing to contact the police. We phoned the police and identified ourselves as the legal executors and they let us into the house where we found her deceased on the bathroom floor. We proceeded to phone the coroner and make arrangements with the mortuary to pick up the remains.

At that moment, we had no understanding of who was going to pay for all of the necessary services. Later we checked the top drawer of her dresser and discovered that she and her late husband, who was a jeweler, jointly owned several mutual funds and money market accounts, as well as real estate holdings amounting to well over one million dollars. We found a deed for the house, which was appraised at $700,000. We also found $20,000 in cash and expensive jewelry. We could not find a will and knew that she had no living relatives. We called a probate estate lawyer and turned the whole matter over to him to dispose of her assets in the manner that the law provided.

To my knowledge none of the accumulated assets of the estate went to any non-profit or medical research. Our church that had basically fed her and provided transportation for the last decade did not receive a dime. To my understanding everything was turned over to the government. This did not come as a surprise or a disappointment, as we were not expecting anything in the first place.

LESSON LEARNED: Our commission as believers in Christ is to continue to keep on freely giving without partiality to everyone who asks, knowing that God is always a good paymaster and He will reward us for our sincere efforts even when someone tries to take unfair advantage.

Humor in Ministry
THE FISH ARE BITING

Over the years, some of my closest friends have been concerned that I was a ministerial workaholic. They believed that I needed to take some periodic rest breaks.

One such break occurred while I was preaching at a church conference on the East Coast. The host pastor asked me to accompany him on a Saturday morning deep sea fishing trip in the Atlantic Ocean. It was a gorgeous day and the tuna were biting almost faster than we could reel them in. It appeared to be one of those days when you could be totally carefree and forget about the rest of the world for a couple of hours.

All of a sudden, we heard the phone on the boat ring. I could overhear the pastor's wife as she frantically shouted at her husband on the other end of the line. "John, don't you know that you have a wedding today? Why are you not here? Where are you?" He said laughingly, "David and I are out deep sea fishing, and I have never seen the tuna biting like they are today! You can do a wedding any day, but this is the best day of fishing I have had this year. I don't know when I am going to get a chance to get out here again."

His wife then asked if he knew who was getting married and why hadn't he remembered. John answered, "I don't recall their names but you can find the information on my desk. I am the senior pastor, and I am delegating this responsibility to you to officiate the wedding today."

After hearing this entire phone conversation, I thought to myself, Pastor John must really be a serious fisherman who loves tuna. When we finally got back on the shore several hours later, he began telling me how he hates fish, particularly tuna. Then he requested that we spread out across the beach and find needy families who would like to take a fish home with them.

LESSONED LEARNED: Everyone has their own priorities and as important as your rest breaks are, you should always make certain that they do not conflict with prior commitments.

CHAPTER 15

Christian Science Reading Room

I N 1970, MY WIFE AND I RECEIVED THE MACEDONIAN
call to return from Canada to co-pastor the church in Oakland that my mother and I had co-founded in 1965. The then elders of the church requested that we come and take over the main leadership for an undetermined season because my mother was suffering from an extended illness and was not, at the time, able to carry on her normal ministerial duties.

Shortly after returning from Canada, it became abundantly clear to us that the church needed to seriously begin searching for new property. The church was bursting at its seams with an influx of new people from almost every Bay Area county. We had totally exceeded our capacity limits, and the overcrowding was extremely dangerous from a safety perspective.

One of the options was to attempt to purchase a Christian Science Reading Room, which we were told was for sale. Often referred to as the Upper Room, it was adjacent to our church parking lot, which was connected to our church facility. The Christian Science property, along with our parking lot, would give us barely enough land to be able to build a new facility that would allow us to triple our capacity as well as build a fellowship hall and some extra teaching rooms.

I approached the Christian Science Reading Room Practitioner who was an elderly woman. She was extremely unreliable and unpredictable. One day she was ready to sell; the next day she would get cold feet and refuse to discuss the matter. Nevertheless, we finally established a bargain price of $25,000. This meant that we would have to take out a loan from the bank, which she unfortunately distrusted and would not do any business with. God then provided a miracle provision. One of our members introduced us to a Cadillac dealer who was willing to give us a brand new, top-of-the-line Cadillac as a tax write-off. Miraculously, we were able to sell the vehicle for the exact same amount that the Christian Scientists were asking for their property. We deposited the money in the bank and began opening escrow in order to complete the proposed property sales transaction.

A week later, I discovered that she had declined the offer because she was not willing to accept a check with the name of a bank on it. After much prayer and consideration, I believe the Holy Spirit prompted me to go to the bank and withdraw $25,000 all in $20 bills. I placed the money in a hardback attaché case and took it over to her house personally. I told her I would leave it with her for one week so she could think it over and recount it as many times as she deemed necessary. I asked her to sign a letter stating that she had received $25,000 in cash with the knowledge that I would be back in seven days to pick it up. At the end of seven days, I went to her house and told her that I was there to pick up the money. She then replied quite indignantly, "Oh no you are not, young man. This is my money!" Suffice it to say, we got the escrow papers signed and were able to tear the building down and begin building our new sanctuary on that property.

LESSON LEARNED: God will use even unconventional means, if necessary, to ensure that His will is accomplished.

Humor in Ministry

HIPPIE BLOWING HIS NOSE

During the late '60s my wife and I pastored a church in Surrey, British Columbia, Canada. The church was very open and welcoming to hippies and those who were part of the drug culture. Many of them had recently come across the U.S. border to avoid the draft, as the Vietnam War was in full swing. The majority of churches at that time were not too accepting of these people. Our church, however, was working closely with Teen Challenge and other outreach ministries where these young men were going through a process of rehabilitation and recovery.

The Jesus Movement, which began in the Bay Area, had not yet spread into Canada. Our church was a place for these men to hang out on Sunday nights. We often geared the service toward outreach and deliverance and sharing testimonies. One Sunday night we were privileged to have a very sophisticated, rather conservative minister as a guest. He was pastor of a large church at the time and was scheduled to be the main speaker of the evening. He was totally against any minister in the pulpit having extra hair, be it facial hair or a ponytail. He preached that this was a sign of rebellion, which the Bible refers to as a sin of witchcraft.

I made the mistake of asking one of our very fervent hippie-type fiery evangelists to give a testimony of his deliverance from the drug culture and all that went along with that lifestyle. I requested that he wear a necktie in respect of the pulpit, especially for our sophisticated guest. In the middle of his very moving presentation, he kind of went off subject and said that he did not have "a clue what this tie is for," and he blew his nose on it several times. I was totally mortified at the time and figured that the service would be a wash, at least at gaining any points with our guest minister. Instead our guest was moved with godly compassion and reached out like a father to this young man, and God used this unseemly, inappropriate nose blowing episode as a point of contact for ministry that might never have happened if there had not been a blowout!

Humor in Ministry

SOCK IT TO ME, LORD!

We have always, throughout the course of our ministry, attempted to maintain a very strict, literal theological interpretation of the Holy Scriptures when administering any of the church sacraments. One Sunday night in our church in Canada we were especially blessed to be baptizing many relatively new converts. The majority of them had been through a number of chemical detox programs, including Teen Challenge, and had a lifelong struggle with addictions.

One of the most memorable candidates was a heroin addict in his early 40s. This weather-beaten man was an older hippie type, who more than likely was a former U.S. draft dodger who had escaped to Canada to receive sanctuary. In the baptismal tank, our pastors attempted to lay hands on him and say the normal prayer of consecration, as well as the Trinitarian Father, Son and Holy Spirit blessing over him. Instead, to our total amazement, he ripped our hands off him, flipped up backwards in the air, yelling, "SOCK IT TO ME, LORD! SOCK IT TO ME, LORD!" as he crashed down under the water without our assistance. Moments later he flew out of the water like a torpedo, totally overcome by the Holy Spirit shouting, "I'm free! I'm free!"

We still firmly believe in correctly administering the right biblical baptismal formula. However, this time, we got quicker and better results because of the sincere heart of this desperate man, than we have, unfortunately, had with some baptismal candidates who merely got wet, after going through a religious ritual. Our former heroin addict studied Christian counseling and set up an alternative Christian detox center so he could "sock it to" those who were seeking freedom from addictions.

CHAPTER 16

Unusual Flying Experiences

OVER THE YEARS, I HAVE HEARD PASTORS QUITE jokingly quote Matthew 28:20: "Lo, I am with you always," with an emphasis on the word "lo" to somehow justify their reluctance to fly on airplanes. If you fly regularly, nationally or internationally, you must be constantly prepared for major delays due to inclement weather, equipment failure, personnel shortages and more recently disputes between the passengers and the crew.

During my last 50+ years of ministry, I have had the opportunity to fly in the majority of the American states as well as 45 nations abroad. I firmly believe that, as a child of God, you have absolutely nothing to fear whether you are in the air or on the ground, if God has some specific assignments that He has for you to yet fulfill. I have been privileged to experience a number of unusual airplane experiences that demonstrate God's protective care.

In my late teens, I was given the opportunity to fly in a pre-WWII, open-air, barnstorming plane with one of the founders of the Latter Rain Movement. It was near his home along the Mexican border in McAllen, Texas. The old relic had a pull starter like a lawn mower. After he got it started, we proceeded to take off and to climb a couple hundred feet—then the engine conked out. Because he could not start it from the inside, we had no other option and crash-landed the airplane. Fortunately, we both got out unscathed. He offered to take me up again later, which I politely declined.

This brought back memories of stories I had heard of my father who was killed in a fiery plane crash in the Royal Canadian Air Force. Little did I know that the ministry God had called me to was going to necessitate that I fly hundreds of thousands of miles around the world on almost every continent.

On one of our mission trips, we were returning from Guangzhou to Hong Kong late one evening in the mid-70s. We had 200 mile per hour headwinds, and it was obviously not advisable to fly under those conditions. However, it was too late to return to Guangzhou, as that airport was closed. The storm clouds appeared to be very threatening, with bursts of thunder and heavy rain. The turbulence kept increasing as we neared Hong Kong. The pilots were having major difficulty landing the plane, and they missed the runway three different times. The Chinese on the plane were terrified and were yelling in Mandarin and English, "We are going to die! We are going to die!" One of our team ministry partners, who was sitting next to me, leaned over and asked in a quivering voice, "How are we supposed to take this?" My spontaneous reply was, "There are three h's: Heaven, Hell, and Hong Kong. We are not going to Hell, so there are only two choices left, Heaven or Hong Kong. So, you might just as well get some sleep and be surprised at which place we wake up in." When we arrived in Hong Kong, our missionary Dennis Balcombe stated quite calmly that a plane the night before had the same scheduled arrival time and went off the runway into the China Sea, "So thank God you made it safely."

On another much less dramatic flight from Las Vegas to Burbank, California, the same principle was illustrated. I boarded a Southwest plane near midnight on a Sunday evening, after an intense weekend of non-stop preaching and prophetic ministry at a church in Las Vegas. When I finally got on the plane, the only seat left was in the back row, across from a loud-mouthed man who appeared to be totally inebriated. The short trip turned out to be very memorable as we experienced an exceptionally bumpy ride en route to Burbank. The drunken man's reaction was very irritating. Every time the plane lost altitude, he started yelling, "Hallelujah, Hallelujah we are going down! Crash and burn, crash and burn, please, Lord, please!" The only thing that I could possibly figure out was that this guy had lost all of the family money gambling and was terrified of having to tell his wife. I figured that he would rather meet the devil than have to talk to her.

I finally told him in no uncertain terms to shut up for the rest of the trip. He asked, "Who are you anyway?" So, I told him that I am a prophet, a man of God, and this plane was not going to go down as long as I was on it because I have some unfulfilled prophecies. I never heard a peep out of him until we landed in Burbank safe and sound.

On another occasion, in 1973, Moses Vegh, an elder from his church and I were flying from the Island of Java back to Jakarta in Indonesia. We had just concluded a week of ministry at a Bible college, which ended with a graduation and commissioning service where a number of students were being sent out to pioneer new ministries in the nation. We boarded an old, antiquated aircraft that I assumed was from the 1940s, with wooden passenger seats and just a little curtain between the pilot in the cockpit and the passenger cabin.

The flight was supposed to be an hour and a half, but was extended nearly five hours. Lightning was dancing off the wings and the plane was barely being held up in the sky. There was a backslidden Pentecostal preacher who was very belligerent and had turned his back completely on God. He was so nervous that he ate his Styrofoam cup and chewed up all of the chicken bones as well. I told him that he had better repent, and if he did not, I would have no other choice than to open up the back door of the plane because he was Jonah and he needed to be thrown overboard so the storm would cease.

He finally got down on his knees on the wooden slats in the floor and chose to get right with God. Tears rolled down his face as he pleaded with God to receive him back into the fold. He appeared to respond out of a godly sorrow, and he stated that regardless of what transpired, he was so happy to feel the presence of God again. About a half hour later, my friend Moses assisted as the copilot and landed the plane. By this time, we had exhausted the fuel and glided the plane into an airport that was shut down for the night.

Moses Vegh often said that God was always in our starts and our stops; perhaps the best example occurred when we were flying from Saigon, Vietnam to Cambodia in early 1973. We were taxiing in on the runway at Phnom Penh Airport on a Transworld Airways plane, when we began to be showered with heavy artillery from enemy fire. The pilots announced that we would be flying out immediately. It seemed that the plane was going straight up out of that war zone. We could actually see the rockets exploding all around our plane as we rapidly climbed to a safe altitude out of range.

In all of these close call encounters, we were thankful that we still had some unfulfilled prophecies. I have often stated from the pulpit that, although I certainly don't desire to die prematurely, I don't wish to be here one minute after God is through with me.

Humor in Ministry
HUMBLING YOURSELF

Throughout my life and ministry, I have often been forced to find out the hard way that if you fail to voluntarily humble yourself on a regular basis, then the Lord will humble you. It

was a revelation to discover that the most spiritually dangerous periods of my life were the times when I was feeling the
best about myself and my secure relationship with the Lord.
I can visibly remember many embarrassing incidents when
I was brought down low under the mighty Hand of God. One
situation took place in 1991, while on a ministry tour that was
head and shoulders above all the rest. I was scheduled to be
one of the evening speakers at a large YWAM conference entitled, "Carry the Light" in Indianapolis, Indiana. The organiz-
ers of the conference requested that I speak on the subject of
evangelizing the inner cities of America.

I remember stating that the racial conflicts, the economic setbacks, the proliferation of drugs and alcohol as well as
political turmoil were all a divine set-up. This indeed was the
set time for the energized Spirit-filled churches of the U.S.
and other nations to step up to the plate and score. The main
thrust of this message, as best as I can recall was, "This Is the
Body of Christ's Finest Hour!" We needed, above all else, to
seize this limited window of opportunity.

The presentation seemed to go remarkably well, and I was
somewhat elated to have been asked to speak for such a large
crowd of several thousand. These enthusiastic young people
were totally sold out. There was also the privilege of being
with some well-known, prestigious leaders.

I thought at the time that this would undoubtedly be one for
the books, and it would certainly be highlighted in my ministry
resume. However, the following day my short 30 minutes of
fame started to fade and go south very quickly. My next ministry assignment was in Nova Scotia, Canada, and, at that time,
there was no direct flight from Indianapolis. In fact, on one of
the layovers of this complicated travel itinerary, I had to hire a
taxi to transport me from where I landed at the domestic airport to the international airport. I was told at the domestic airport information desk that the international airport was only
about five miles away. They said that it should not take more

that 10-15 minutes at the most to get there. I was directed to the first taxi in line and the driver put my luggage in the trunk. When I got in the car, I told the driver, who appeared to speak very little English, that I needed to go to the international airport as quickly as possible as my flight would be leaving soon. The driver immediately took off driving very fast, far over the speed limit. It seemed obvious that he must have gotten my message even though he did not speak a word to me. Twenty minutes later there was no airport in sight, and I mistakenly asked the driver if he was going the right way. He appeared to be very visibly annoyed, but nonetheless, he kept going, saying nothing. Another 15 minutes went by, and there was still no airport in sight. We were getting further and further out into the boonies. I asked him again if he thought we were going the right way.

At that moment and much to my surprise, he went into a major rage. He stopped the taxi and ordered me to get out. He opened the trunk and threw all my luggage onto the ground into a mud hole. He told me that he was carrying a gun and that I had better quickly empty my wallet and give him all the cash, which amounted to a few hundred dollars, so that he would not be forced to use the gun on me. Of course, I immediately complied and gave him all the money I had. He got back into his taxi and sped off leaving me penniless by the side of the road.

I found one of those old-time pay phones, called the police and made a report of the whole incident. The officer on the other end of the line told me that they probably could not do very much to help me because in the process of being so terrified by this robbery, I had failed to get the name of the taxicab company and the license of the car or even a good description of the driver. Nevertheless, the policeman told me to stay at the pay phone, and he would call a taxi company that takes credit cards to come and pick me up and take me to the international airport. When I finally arrived at the airport, I was greatly relieved to find that my plane had been delayed a couple of hours, and I still had ample time to make the flight.

I could not help but reflect back to the exciting night before, when I had been tremendously elated with the rare opportunity to address a large crowd and feeling like a celebrity of sorts. Now, a day later I was reduced to nothing more than an unknown mugged individual who had been robbed by a taxi driver and left penniless by the side of the road en route to my next ministry assignment.

LESSON LEARNED: Don't think more highly of yourself than the facts would suggest. Remember that if you fail to humble yourself regularly, God will.

CHAPTER 17

Isn't Grace Amazing?

G ALATIANS 6:9 SAYS THAT WE ARE NOT TO GROW WEARY
in well doing for we will reap in due season if we faint
not. This, in essence, means that if we persist and are
unwilling to give up or throw in the towel, we will get the desired results.

In 2 Timothy 2:1, the Apostle Paul's final farewell words to
his surrogate son in the faith, Timothy, were to be strong in
grace. This involves possessing patience and longsuffering
with difficult, unlikeable people, where grace becomes a necessary component. This chapter contains three stories that il-
lustrate just how amazing grace can be.

THE ANGEL OF HOSPITALITY WHO REFUSED TO GIVE UP

Years ago, we were highly favored to have a godly lady in our
assembly whom I would like to refer to as the angel of hospitality. She was as beautiful on the inside as she was on the outside. Her warm, gracious, welcoming attitude made ladies of
all different strata and stages of life very comfortable and at
home in her immaculately kept house. She was a superb cook
and stellar baker who always prepared food fit for royalty.

Those blessed to be invited to her home always left with a
generous package to take with them. My mother, a gifted Bible teacher, conducted impartational teaching sessions for a

number of years in her home during the height of the Charismatic Movement. Scores of women from all over the Bay Area testified of receiving the baptism of the Holy Spirit, as well as miraculous healings and financial provision during these sessions.

Others witnessed to the fact that major transformation took place in their marriages and families, as a result of the intercessory prayer sessions that also transpired at these gatherings. However, in the midst of all of those sovereign God-encounters, our angel of hospitality bore a deep inward sorrow and hurt.

This was rarely detectable in her joyful, upbeat demeanor. Her husband was a highly successful businessman who had a major alcohol problem, even though he had apparently followed in the ways of the Lord in days gone by. He was able to mask it pretty well most of the time, but he had also been known to have extramarital affairs. On at least one occasion he kicked his wife out of their bed in order to accommodate another woman.

Many people including those closest to her strongly suggested that enough was enough, and it was time for her to escape this horrible situation. She was quite aware of the fact that from a biblical standpoint, she was not obligated to put up with this kind of emotional abuse and torture any longer. However, she stated clearly that God had dropped a word of assurance in her heart that He would give her the grace to endure and that she would witness her husband returning to God before he died.

Several years went by, and things appeared to be worsening; however, this gracious angel of hospitality refused to give up. She kept holding on to the Word and was unwilling to cast away her confidence, no matter what people said or what she was being put through.

A couple of weeks before he died, her husband came down to the altar of our church in the middle of a Sunday morning service. He was visibly shaken and looked very weak and frail. We stopped the whole service and several hundred people publicly witnessed this man openly repenting to his wife for all the hurt, pain and suffering he had put her through. He then wept his way back to God, hands were laid on him and he received the baptism of the Holy Spirit. All of this transpired as an open witness to everyone present. Here was someone who was unwilling to put her own needs ahead of a person needing redemption, a person she loved.

This also spoke very clearly to me of the fact that you can never question the degree of grace that God gives to another person. Nor can you question another person's journey where grace was lifted, and God led them to go in an entirely different direction. Our angel of hospitality refused to give up, and God rewarded her accordingly.

Isn't grace amazing?

A RAW LOVEFEST IN SAN FRANCISCO SUPERIOR COURT

Hebrews 4:18 makes reference to the fact that there is a special measure of grace that can only be released in the time of need. Although we ourselves cannot store grace in a capsule or in a vault in advance, God always and freely dispenses His grace during those challenging seasons when life appears to be spinning out of control.

Tom Burnoski and his family, long-time members of our church, have certainly gone through more than their fair share of extremely painful, tragic experiences. They have learned firsthand that Christianity is not the charmed life, nor one that causes its adherents to avoid hardship, trouble and loss. Rather, Christianity enables a believer to stand tall and remain firm and levelheaded whenever sorrow and bereavement meet us head-on, and there is absolutely no place to lean but on the everlasting arms. It is in times like these that we must fully rely on the assurance that God's grace is totally sufficient for us.

Our story begins with Tiffany Faith, the Burnoskis' beautiful 20-year-old daughter, who had been attending California

State University Fullerton to become a civil engineer, which at the time was not a career path to which young women aspired.

On April 6, 2013, Tiffany's sweetheart, Casey, was driving Tiffany and two of her siblings, 5-year-old Elizabeth and 12-year-old Matthew, to their brother's baseball game. Heading north on Highway 5, Casey fell asleep at the wheel.

When he woke up, he discovered that the car was off the shoulder of the highway. He tried desperately to compensate, but by then, the car was out of control. When he attempted to get it back on the freeway, it flipped over at least five times in mid-air. The observers in the other cars at the scene thought it must have been staged as a Hollywood stunt. It was a totally horrifying experience, and the children in the car said that it sounded like a bomb had exploded in the car, as they witnessed their beloved sister being killed on impact.

Tom and his brokenhearted family made a conscious decision to forgive Casey and to extend grace to him despite the pain of this horrible accident. Tom still visits Tiffany's graveside weekly, four years later. It was absolutely impossible to imagine that anything more could ever happen to bring increased devastation to Tom and his family.

Tom had been employed by the City of San Francisco since 2006 as a lead gardener in the Mission District of the Bernal Heights at Holly Park. This park was known for being like a suburban retreat in the midst of the heavily populated city. On an eventful day in September 2013, the same year that Tiffany was killed, Tom was driving downhill in the park in his designated city-owned truck, en route to his office to sign out for the day, when he ran over what he thought was a dog.

When he got to his office, he reported the accident to his boss. It was not until the next day, after Tom had been booked overnight into jail, that he found out from the police that he had actually run over and killed a lady who was resting on the grass near a tree. She had not been visible to him. Fortunately, her baby who was with her escaped the accident.

The police investigator told Tom that he should immediately obtain the best defense lawyer possible. The investigator stated that this incident was being blasted all over the Bay Area as a lead story in the media. Tom was released on bail, which miraculously continued until the day of his final sentencing almost four years later.

His eldest daughter, Jamie, a committed believer and worship leader, had a contact through the Jewish school where she worked, who connected her father with a highly qualified defense attorney by the name of Robert Wagner. This man proved to be a godsend, as he had the respect of all the judges, as well as many others within the legal community. A benevolent friend put up the first $10,000 retainer in order to set the case in motion. A few months later, Attorney Wagner told Tom to come up with another $10,000 or else it would be necessary for him to drop the case, as it was going to require an extensive amount of work. Tom then sold his truck, exhausted all of his assets and was forced to move with his three teenaged boys into a friend's home in order to pay the attorney the $10,000. Miracle of miracles, Attorney Wagner was so touched by Tom's case after he found out that he had sold his truck, that he never charged Tom another cent for the rest of the case.

Tom was charged with two felonies, which remained in effect until the time of the final sentencing. Upon the advice of the attorney, Tom did approximately 1,500 hours of documented voluntary community service, which was presented to the presiding judge. In the meantime, there were a number of regular hearings, which were undergirded with the prayers of scores of people. They were believing that God would grant Tom some mercy and that the charges would be reduced from two felonies to two misdemeanors. At one of the later hearings, it was stated that putting Tom in prison would not be helpful to him or his family and would not bring any relief for the victim's family.

Many people supported Tom at the final sentencing: Tom's oldest daughter and two of his sons, Jonathan and Joshua;

Shiloh's Executive Pastor, Chris Casimere; Elder Lori King; the boys' baseball coach, Javier, and his daughter and I were all in the courtroom.

Near the beginning of the proceedings, the victim's husband was asked to speak, and he said in effect, "Tom, you killed my wife and as horribly painful as that is, I am a changed man. When I reviewed my life, I realized that I have done some dumb things and have, on occasion, driven recklessly and could have killed somebody myself. Tom, I forgive you."

Tom reached out to shake his hand, but instead the victim's husband hugged him. At that moment, I could not help but recall the fact that Tom and his family had chosen to do the very same thing to forgive Casey, the driver of the car who was responsible for killing their daughter. Matthew 5:7 states that whenever you extend mercy or grace, it is returned back to you.

The victim's sister then got up and said, in essence, that she had been working on forgiveness, but was not quite there yet. However, she would continue working on it as her mother had encouraged her to keep striving to forgive. Apparently, the original judge who had presided over the case had retired; he had left detailed instructions for the presiding judge, which included the reducing of the two felonies to two misdemeanors. The presiding judge said that he would now attach the legal instructions as part of the permanent records for the case. He then stated that this was, on the one hand, one of the most tragic experiences he had ever witnessed on the bench. However, it was a once-in-a-lifetime experience to be present to see both parties forgiving and releasing one another. He then concluded his statement by saying, "There is so much love in this room."

As we left the courtroom, people were shaking hands and hugging one another on both sides of the case. Coach Javier, the boys' baseball coach, said that the atmosphere was so charged by the power of God in the room that, in his words, he actually felt like his body was going to explode. Tom's daughter

Jamie said that she felt like she had been in a heavenly worship service. Pastor Chris said that this whole ordeal was an unexpected raw lovefest. He stated, in effect, that you should be able to experience this at church, but it doesn't happen often because people don't always practice their Christianity as they should.

As for me, I could not help but say that although we were all believing God for a positive outcome, we were all taken off guard by the extent of love, mercy and grace that was visibly manifested in that courtroom. This unmerited favor was released that day when it was so desperately needed as God showed up with a package marked, "Isn't Grace Amazing?"

REDEMPTION IN THE STREETS

The Pharisees' greatest indictment against Jesus was that He was always hanging around the wrong crowd. He was a friend of sinners. Often He was the chief guest at their parties, because He would invariably spice up the atmosphere with an unexpected miracle. He would publicly debate with the religious crowd.

Religious people can be extremely heartless and fruitless; they will write off anyone who doesn't measure up to their rigid legalistic standards. Grace is a door opened for people who feel they have failed beyond redemption and who experience and endure the rejection and condemnation that is often heaped upon them by the religious world.

Evangelist Eloise Carey can be affectionately referred to as a crowned queen of the unpredictable. Frequently Eloise would go to challenging hotspots where she would set up her portable keyboard and PA system. Then she would begin to aggressively call down the heavenly presence of God through her ground shaking music and her loud, booming yet melodious voice. One day she was out cruising the neighborhood close to the church, when she felt the Holy Spirit draw her attention to a house where she could minister just a short distance from an elementary school. She said it appeared there was a constant flow of illegal drug activity going on around the clock. This was clearly a direct threat to the children and neighbors in the community.

To Eloise this was a divine appointment, ripe for the picking, and she refused to be intimidated. She went straight up to the door and spoke with the owner of the house, which happened to be an elderly woman, and received permission to plug her system into the electric outlet in the home. Eloise immediately began playing and singing anointed and upbeat worship songs as well as old-time, soul-convicting gospel hymns at the top of her lungs. Her piercing voice reverberated throughout the surrounding community.

The young men who were responsible for perpetrating this drug invasion into the community were extremely irritated and told Eloise that she had absolutely no right to be there as this was their turf. Nevertheless, she refused to be run off or silenced, but rather she kept coming back day after day with increased boldness. She not only continued singing, but also began preaching the gospel and sharing God's love throughout the community. Many people came out to support her.

In a few days, a San Francisco-based television network brought their truck, fully equipped to record her, which allowed the good news of the gospel to go out throughout the entire San Francisco Bay Area. As a result of this bold action of faith, the whole surrounding neighborhood was positively affected by her ministry.

Shortly after, the police came and closed down the whole drug operation, and the house was sold. Most importantly, people's lives were changed forever as grace was being released.

On another occasion, this fiery evangelist was impacted by a message that I gave at the church on the subject of communion. In the message, I stated that if communion was nothing more than a once a month religious ritual, then it was something that should be discontinued because it was doing an injustice to the redemptive power of the blood of Jesus.

Most of the parishioners no doubt thought that this was another great inspirational message, and perhaps they should at least pick up a copy of the CD at the end of the service at the media booth, just in case they get around to listening to it again. Others were taking it much more seriously, claiming healing and deliverance, and even a protective covering of the blood over their families and communities.

However, Eloise, with her Holy Ghost sanctified imagination, envisioned a communion message being activated in the streets. She believed that it needed to be taken to those who never darkened the door of a church. She had a passion to expose them to the real non-condemning Jesus, whose blood was just as powerful to deliver them, as it was anyone in the church. This time she not only set up her keyboard and sound equipment, but she also set up a communion table complete with the elements of the bread and the wine. The location was in front of a pizza parlor near a bar in a small shopping center on International Boulevard in East Oakland. The end result was that many unbelievers and backsliders were drawn to the redemptive power of God as she had them kneel before the communion table in order to be reclaimed.

Soon the pizza parlor, which had been known for a long time as a place where illegal drugs were passed, was closed and forced out of business as another neighborhood was impacted by the blood of Jesus. It is God's desire to raise up a church within the church that is being awakened to the fact that there are millions of AWOL former Christians who have lost their way in this nation, and they will never be able to find God in a performance-based religious ritualistic environment.

There are true believers like Eloise who are willing to look beyond the faults and failings of our broken world and are willing to be sacrificially inconvenienced in order to throw out a lifeline of God's grace through demonstrating His love and acceptance to people who most others easily reject.

Isn't Grace Amazing?

PART III

Outreach to City and Nation

In 1964, my mother, Dr. Violet Kiteley, and I, two Caucasian missionaries, emigrated from Canada to the tumultuous region of the San Francisco/Oakland Bay Area. This was during the height of the Civil Rights Movement, the Vietnam War protests, the hippie/ flower children revolution, The Jesus Movement and The Charismatic Movement. God graced us during the turbulent era to establish a multicultural, multi-racial, multi-generational ministry, which continued to thrive over five decades later with congregants from over 50 nations.

In Part III the reader will discover that the story continues to unfold as this ministry employs God-given strategies, which have left a lasting mark on the city, region and nation.

CHAPTER 18

How Shiloh's Food Ministry Began

Aᴼᴼ FTER OUR CHURCH MOVED TO ITS PRESENT LOCATION in Oakland, California, we soon discovered that our new district had statistically one of the highest rates of domestic crime as well as burglaries and robberies in the city. In the beginning days at the new location, they reported a number of break-ins and robberies. One day an Oakland Police Department captain made an appointment to come and talk with me and one of our elders to discuss this whole matter of crime in the neighborhood.

He stated that it was possible for a church to become nothing more than an island in a neighborhood and that many churches were totally out of touch with their community. The officer strongly hinted that we were in that same category. Evidently a growing number of churches had congregations that were commuting from other parts of the city as well as other cities in the region. These churches had little or no connection to the community where they were located. He finally got our attention when he stated, "If you are not planning to give items away, then they will literally come and take it."

With this thought-provoking challenge, we decided it was time to take action. We purchased a non-operating gas station a block away from the church and began a food ministry to test this theory for ourselves. The officer said that there many seniors in the community who didn't have enough food to get through the month. Their Social Security checks usually ran out before the last week of the month. He said that if we would supply this segment of the neighborhood with food, the church would be protected from burglaries and robberies. He said that the church would be under the watchful eye of the sons and grandsons who live in the neighborhood who would stand guard, informing the perpetrators of crime, "This is my grandma's church, and she gets her groceries there and attends other programs. So you best not mess with that place, if you know what is good for you!"

We soon discovered that this theory, by and large, worked extremely well, and we have had a minimum of break-ins and losses from that time until this day.

During the Y2K scare, I was asked to participate in a panel presentation with a number of clergy including a representative from the Oakland Mormon church. He suggested that our church and their church were very similar, inasmuch as we both were involved with food storage. My reply was that there was one major difference and that was that our church gives food to anyone who is hungry regardless of race, creed, religion or even financial status, and, as far as I knew, their church only stored food for their own members. One day, some of our food distribution volunteers phoned me, very perturbed, because there was a man there who wanted to pick up food, and he was driving a brand new, top-of-the-line Mercedes Benz. I asked them to let me handle it, and I went and talked with the man. I found that he had been sent there by a social service agency to get food for a family that had just been burned out of their home and had lost everything.

LESSON LEARNED: Don't be too quick to judge. If you don't plan to give it away, they will take it anyway. But more importantly, as a church we are called to fulfill the mandate in Matthew 25, which says, "If you do it unto the least of these my brethren, you have done it unto Me."

CHAPTER 19
Pleitner Street

ONE SATURDAY IN THE EARLY '80s, WHILE I WAS preparing my Sunday message about going beyond our four walls and ministering with merciful compassion, I received a phone call from a non-Christian landlord who owned several apartment complexes on Pleitner Street, four blocks from our church.

The man was greatly alarmed by the spike in crime, including murder, in the area, as well as the recent influx of drugs and drug dealers, which were invading the Oakland neighborhood. This had caused both young and old to lock themselves like hostages in their own apartments in order to hide from these intruders. He had heard that our church was involved in a holistic ministry including exorcism. He specifically requested that the church send a team of ministers on a Saturday to come down to Pleitner Street and exorcise the neighborhood. I was quite honestly not too enthused with this proposition because it was a fairly demanding task on a Saturday, which I had dedicated to study, rest and family time.

In my mind, this kind of spiritual warfare and exorcism belonged strictly behind the doors of the church in a designated prayer area or office. I had believed that we needed to declare our spiritual authority over the powers of darkness from the church platform. Nevertheless, I reluctantly agreed, and we got a permit to close off Pleitner Street and set up a stage.

On Sundays, our choir and worship team had sang songs about conquering the enemy, not realizing that we had been totally isolated and insulated from the people who needed us the most. We had done very little to address the devastation that was just four blocks from our building. We were now being challenged to not only do the church on Sunday, in our comfortable sanctuary, but now to become the church to our neighbors.

That Saturday we painted a house, repaired a fence, barbecued food and gave away tons of groceries and new and used clothing. We had tables that provided health and job information, with support from our church and Oakland City Council members. Our pastors preached powerful and convicting gospel messages.

Near the end of the day, we asked the neighbors to join hands in a unified prayer of solidarity, and we declared Pleitner Street and the surrounding streets to be off-limits to the powers of darkness, which had manifested itself in drug dealing, murder and domestic violence. I was told that everyone in that four-block area participated in that united action, including some of the main drug dealers and kingpins who obviously had no clue of what God was about to do through this spiritual encounter.

Truthfully, I was glad that this day had come to a close, even though it was extremely successful. We could now get back to our primary obligation of ministering to each other within the four walls of our church. Little did I know that we were about to embark on a whole new area of ministry, which would involve taking evangelism and worship to the streets of Oakland.

After a few days, we received a phone call from the Commander of the Community Services Division of the Oakland Police Department who had worked very closely with us during the outreach. He stated that whatever we did on Pleitner Street we needed to take to the hotspots and high crime areas throughout the City of Oakland. Apparently, we had made headlines in the *New York Times* and were being featured by several local and national television and radio news outlets under the storyline "Taking Your City Back, Block by Block."

Pleitner Street had become a successful model from which a movement was started—a movement that brought the Word, worship and practical resources to the streets through block parties held in neighborhoods throughout the city.

Many Oakland neighborhoods reported a reduction in crime and drugs, and we worked with the Oakland Police Community Services Division to establish a neighborhood watch. This effort lasted for many years and was later picked up by my daughter, Melinda, in an afterschool program known as Jungle Jam, which she led for ten years. This consisted of a sidewalk Sunday school program where hundreds of kids assembled and made commitments to Jesus.

Over time, our Outreach Ministry has evolved into new areas of ministry even as the commission remains the same—to become available to the people who need us the most, lest we become irrelevant. The primary call of the church is not just to disciple the congregation but rather to disciple them with an end goal or purpose, which is to inspire, empower, equip and release the so-called rank and file to fulfill their individual calling and to exercise their gifts both inside and outside of the church.

CHAPTER 20

Being an Advocate— Reverend Betita Coty

G OD'S INTENTION IS NOT TO JUST LIFT US UP TO ANOTHER level personally, but it is His desire that we always take others with us. This is to ensure that the Kingdom of God always succeeds. Our greatest season of reaping transpires after we have freely given to people who have absolutely no possibility of reciprocating back to us. In Proverbs 31:8-9, the Message translation says to "Speak up for the people who have no voice, for the rights of all the down-and-outers. Speak out for justice! Stand up for the poor and destitute!" The Living Bible paraphrase says, "Defend those who cannot help themselves. Yes, speak up for the poor and helpless." Such was the influential life and ministry of Reverend Betita Coty, the most unique staff member that we ever hired at Shiloh Church. She was never concerned about being politically correct or operating by any so-called protocol. And she would never, under any circumstance, take no for an answer. She firmly believed in bridging the gap between the people who had financial resources and training and those who were disenfranchised and didn't know how to connect with the system. This unconventional, radical lady would go anywhere, at any time and at any cost to ensure that the Kingdom of God was expanded and multiplied.

One Saturday evening at about 8 p.m., my then teenager son Patrick called me collect in a hysterical voice from an old-style pay phone in Tijuana, Mexico. Reverend Betita Coty had taken our son along with her son on a whirlwind missions excursion. It was her hope that the boys would get a fresh appreciation of just how good they had it in America, and perhaps they would even catch a missionary vision while they were on this trip. My son stated that Betita had been illegally preaching on the streets with a bullhorn near the plaza, was arrested and taken to the police station for questioning and possibly booked into the Mexican jail. He told me that they had very little money, and he pleaded for me to come from Oakland, 600+ miles away, on a Saturday evening and bring them home. He told me that they were sitting outside on a bench. Soon it would be dark, and they felt very unsafe. I got the number of the pay phone, and I told him I would call him back as soon as I figured out what we needed to do. In just a few moments, I received a call back from my son telling me that Betita was released from the police station, and was back out, preaching illegally, after she had been severely warned not to use a bullhorn in the streets again.

I prevailed upon my son to go and stop Betita and get her on the phone. As her pastor, I told her that she needed to quit preaching and start heading for the border immediately. She reluctantly listened to me, quoting all kinds of scriptures, such as "Woe unto me if I preach not the gospel." Within a few moments, the Mexican police were there and told her the same thing I told her, that she needed to leave the country. The positive outcome was that both boys got to witness what a serious Christian in action looks like. She did not just talk about her willingness to go to jail—she did it.

Another Betita Coty experience occurred when I was watching the six o'clock news and saw our church van bearing a sign that read, "Shiloh Christian Fellowship, a church that loves God and loves people." Betita was behind the wheel, and she was going back and forth on the TV screen, driving on the sidewalk near the San Francisco City Hall. Apparently, the San Francisco police and fire departments were in the process of hosing down the homeless tents that were pitched out in front of the city hall. The people staying there had been given multiple warnings to move out of the area but of course had nowhere to go. Betita, true to her calling as a bold, uncompromising advocate for those without a voice, was speaking out on their behalf. She was using our church van to attempt to block the fire department staff, who were trying to dismantle the homeless encampment. All the local news stations were out there, and the church was front and center in the news. That night Betita negotiated with the city officials to have the homeless people moved into a temporary homeless shelter, which was property that the city owned. She also got them to promise that they would provide more permanent shelters for these homeless people in the future. The question is, what would have happened had Betita not been there as a mediator between the City of San Francisco and the homeless who were in the process of being displaced?

This fearless, 90-pound, fiery, Latin evangelist regularly confronted drug dealers, who were two and three times her size, at various Saturday block parties that Shiloh and I sponsored. These block parties were organized to convene at hotspots around the city of Oakland, in cooperation with the Community Services Division of the Oakland Police Department, and the mayor would often attend.

After being tipped off by the Oakland Police Department, Betita would stand up with us on the back of a rented flatbed truck and, on a few occasions, would call out the addresses over the PA system where illegal drug activity was transpiring. She then would order these drug dealers to quit being cowards and to come out of their houses and meet us on the stage in front of hundreds of people. There were often police officers and politicians in the crowd. She would then inform them, with her heavy accent, that they were responsible for holding the youth and the elderly hostage in their homes in this community. She said, "Mr. Drug Dealer, we are not going to tolerate this any longer." She was going to work with her attorneys to get their homes red-stickered and cars impounded if they persisted in continuing this drug activity. She then told them they needed to get down on their knees and repent and say the sinner's prayer, which some did quite sheepishly. Time and eternity will only reveal the harvest that came forth from proclaiming the gospel in both songs from our choir and words from our ministers. This ministry happened almost weekly for over a decade.

During the late '90s Betita Coty decided to camp out in a tent across the street from the administration building of the Oakland public schools. She fasted for over 26 days for the reforms that were needed for the public-school children of Oakland. I and many other pastors tried to prevail upon her to end the fast, as it was taking a tremendous toll on her body. She was extremely weak and frail and was suffering with terminal cancer. She was willing to lay her life down for the school children of Oakland. Her sincere efforts as a radical advocate were inadvisable according to many people, but they resulted in much-needed changes in the educational system, including the ending of the teacher strike on the 26th day of Betita's fast.

A couple months later, Betita invited my wife and me to her home to plan her funeral. She had already invited the mayor, some city council members and local news anchors to attend, and had given specific messages that she wanted them to share at her home-going service. She also gave me a complete script and clearly stated that if I didn't say it the way she wanted, she would sit up in her casket and correct me publicly! She was obviously a woman who knew exactly what she wanted, and also knew how to get the city officials and media to comply with her wishes, including following her around to whatever event she was participating in. She somehow had learned the art of "working the system." Like the legendary Robin Hood, she knew how to negotiate with the rich in order to give to the disenfranchised and disinherited people of the Bay Area.

Betita passed away on August 31, 1996. She will never be forgotten. Betita Coty's ministry of advocacy continues to live on.

CHAPTER 21

Washington for Jesus

G OD HAS REPEATEDLY BROUGHT ABOUT A SPIRITUAL revival accompanied by social, economic and political change whenever His people respond to a prophetic call for repentance and unification.[9] There is perhaps no better example of this than what transpired on the Washington D.C. National Mall when 750,000 people from all denominations and racial backgrounds assembled from every state in the union as well as from over 100 nations to intercede on behalf of America and our world at that time.

All this began in the summer of 1978 at Shiloh Church's annual family camp in Santa Cruz, California. Pastor John Gimenez and his wife, Anne, cofounders of Rock Church in Virginia Beach, were the principal speakers at the camp. Pastor Gimenez was preaching one of his classic messages on how the psalmist David waged war against his nine-and-a-half foot, ruthless opponent, Goliath. He stated emphatically that David did not aim his stone at Goliath's feet, or his stomach or his chest, but he went directly for his head. He said that the only

---

9. Thus, 2 Chronicles 7:13–14 provides: "If I shut up the heavens so that there is no rain, or if I command the locust to devour the land or if I send pestilence among My people, and My people who are called by My name humble themselves and pray and seek My face and turn from their wicked ways, then I will hear from heaven, will forgive their sin and will heal their land."

possible way that the church could become effective again in the nation was if we aimed directly at the head.

It was at that moment that my mother, Pastor Violet Kiteley, and I were prompted by the Holy Spirit to give Pastor Gimenez a very specific word of prophetic wisdom and direction, which set into action the word that had been given in the message. The word, in essence, stated that the church desperately needed to rise up in a unified fashion and gather together from across the nation in order that they might humble themselves and pray a prayer of repentance so that God will heal our land one more time.

The next thing that spontaneously transpired in that comparatively small service with just several hundred people was that we elected Pastor Gimenez to be the Chairman of what was later to be known as "Washington for Jesus." This was later unanimously confirmed by many notable Christian statesmen[10] who wholeheartedly signed on for this enormous task, which took two years of intense planning and a couple million dollars seed money for it to become a reality.

There is often a huge cost to carrying out the prophetic word. The decade of the '80s had begun on a somber note with 52 Americans being held hostage at the American Embassy in Iran. On the home front, the nation was experiencing inflation and recession at the same time. According to the *Los Angeles Times*, most savings and loan organizations were charging 17–18 percent interest on home mortgages and the prime rate was over 21 percent. The American dream turned into the American nightmare; there were long gas lines, and you could only purchase gas every other day depending on whether your license plate number was odd or even. Often

---

10. Pat Robertson, founder of the Virginia Beach-based Christian Broadcasting Network, and Bill Bright of Campus Crusade were chosen program co-chairmen, with Pastor Gimenez chosen as the national chairman. Pat Robertson said the 1980 rally "completely shifted the political landscape and the religious landscape of this country."

when you finally got up to the pumps several hours later, they had run out of fuel.

On April 24, 1980, an ill-fated military operation to rescue the 52 American hostages held in Tehran ended with eight U.S. servicemen dead and no hostages rescued. The Iranians used the charred remains of those killed as a backdrop for their news releases. The nation was rocked and humiliated by these events, which occurred one week before the Washington for Jesus rally. This desecration on top of the previous decade's price freezes, Watergate and the Vietnam War, had left the national morale at an all-time low.

There was a sense of hopelessness, but there was also an understanding that the only solution was for the nation to humble itself and return to God. Washington for Jesus was scheduled for April 29, 1980. That day was specifically chosen for its historical significance; it was the anniversary of the 1607 planting of the cross by Robert Hunt, chaplain of the Jamestown Colony, in dedication to the country's first settlement. On April 29, 1980, low-hanging rain clouds and forecasted thunderstorms with cloudbursts threatened to put a major damper on this event. By noon, a huge gathering of over 750,000 poured onto the Washington, D. C. Mall. It was one of the largest Christian gatherings up until that time.

There were hundreds of chartered buses and planes, and people came on trains and District of Columbia public transit. All began arriving and assembling on the Mall. This huge, closely packed crowd of participants was made up of Evangelicals and Charismatics, as well as Catholics. They were from both major political parties. It looked like a sea of people stretching from the Capitol Building to the Washington Monument. Not since the 1976 Bicentennial celebrations had there been such a gathering on the National Mall.

We had not come to listen to any political speeches or to hear from any candidates who were running for office, even though it was an election year. We were not assembled there to condemn or denounce anyone. We were going there solely to point the finger at ourselves and sincerely repent before God for our own personal failures, particularly in light of the fact that there were numerous religious scandals by high profile television celebrities. We were there to pray for our nation and for the reconciliation of the Lord's church worldwide.

At 6 in the morning, Pastor Gimenez went to the microphone and there was a thunderous sound of praise as well as intercession for the weather. Those who were there can attest to the fact that almost instantaneously the clouds began to clear, the rain ceased and we enjoyed a beautiful day with temperatures in the 70s even though the National Weather Service maps showed heavy clouds and rain completely surrounding the Washington D.C. area. It was like we were in the Land of Goshen that day, and we were enjoying the sunlight while the rest of the region was experiencing stormy weather.

We gave out hundreds of thousands of cans of non-perishable goods, which the participants brought, to the homeless. This enormous prayer meeting lasted 12 solid hours. There were seven days and nights of continuous praise and prayer and worship on the Mall, which began with a youth concert led by Reverend Bart Pierce on April 28 and lasted through the National Day of Prayer on May 5.

A number of notable miracles transpired directly as a result of this gigantic prayer meeting, in 1980 and subsequently in each Washington for Jesus meeting that convened every eight years through 2004, as well in as other prayer gatherings organized by numerous Christian organizations.

A partial listing of these miracles includes:

There was a breaking down of the walls of partition, distrust and lack of fellowship between Evangelicals, Pentecostals and Charismatics. This began a new fellowship, which still continues to this day.

At that time, a megachurch might have 1,000 members. Today, megachurches often have upwards of 10,000 members.

Tremendous revivals have occurred in Asia, Africa and South America, which have affected entire nations.

Pastor David Schoch, a noted prophetic voice, gave a very relevant word from the Lord as we were leaving Washington, D.C. in 1980. He stated that God had, on that day, April 29, given the initiative back into the hands of the church. And he stated that we were all to see that we did not relinquish it.

I am sorry to say that the church in America today needs a fresh new prophetic call to humility, repentance and unification so that God can once again restore His fractured apathetic Body, which is supposed to be a shining light set up on a hill. May our prayer be that our lawless, disoriented society, particularly the youth of this nation, will be revisited by God and that His people will quit "doing church" and again actually *become* the church that He has called us to be.

CHAPTER 22

March for Righteousness

IT DOESN'T TAKE ANY SUPERNATURAL INSIGHT OR DISCERNMENT to conclude we are living in a post-Christian era in America. There are very few, if any, givens or absolutes or firm convictions. It appears to be like the time in the Book of Judges when every man did that which was right in his own eyes. Social media, with all of its positive features, has seemingly made lots of uninformed individuals into instant experts on almost every subject imaginable. It appears that real, uncompromising Christians are very often considered judgmental bigots, and they are increasingly marginalized and often ridiculed. As their voices are being silenced, they are primarily losing their prophetic voice. In every generation, Christians need to stand up and be counted in matters of social justice, fairness and righteousness. This has to be done with a true spirit of grace and humility, and our message needs to be one that is redemptive, presenting a viable, hopeful alternative.

In the late fall of 1986, a coalition of churches in Oakland attempted to respond in a righteous manner to the event of the Felix Mitchell funeral, which had gained national and international notoriety. Wikipedia describes his funeral as follows:

Thousands of people, including many youth, lined the streets to pay homage and respect to Felix Mitchell, who had been responsible for pouring millions of dollars' worth

143

of heroin and cocaine into Oakland, CA and the surrounding region annually. He was convicted in 1985 and sentenced to life in prison at Leavenworth Federal Penitentiary, where he was fatally stabbed just two days before his 32nd birthday. His funeral procession consisted of his body being carried through the streets by a horse-driven carriage trailed by 14 Rolls-Royce limousines. This celebratory outpouring honoring a drug lord in such a royal fashion was a vivid example of the impact that drugs, as well as the drug culture, was having on the youth at the time.

It was high time for the churches, non-profits and residents of the city that desired to join us, to stand up and be counted. The coalition was led by the pastor of Allen Temple Baptist Church, Dr. J. Alfred Smith Sr., and myself. Scores of other churches from various denominations, parachurch groups and many other non-profits were involved as well. It is estimated that 12,000 people, which was the largest march in Oakland since the civil rights era, marched through the streets. The march started at Allen Temple Baptist Church on 86th Ave. and International Blvd. and concluded at the City Hall in downtown Oakland. We were led by the Oakland Police Department and had a large flatbed truck with singers and musicians from Shiloh and other churches. As the police indicated where the hotspots of drug activity were, we would stop the march and appoint one of the pastors to lead us in prayer, that the drug dealing and crime would cease in that area. It was no doubt pretty intimidating for the people in those houses and apartments to see thousands of hands raised toward their residence in prayer. When we arrived at Broadway St., downtown, there was a gathering of hundreds of people. There was also a substantial crowd already awaiting us at City Hall that consisted largely of individuals unable to march long distances who had come on public transportation to join us. The day climaxed with a brief rally at City Hall consisting of prayers and speeches from clergy, local politicians and representatives from Sacramento. All in all, at the end of the day, it was a very gratifying and unifying experience. A lot of goodwill was established, and many of the groups decided to network in their community to bring about change. One of our council members Leo Bazile asked the question, "Where are CBS and NBC?" considering the fact they had all showed up for the drug lord's funeral. It was reported that within the next couple of weeks, some high-profile drug lords who openly violated and evaded the laws for over a decade were arrested.

The major lesson that I learned from the March for Righteousness effort and other events we participated in, is that it is relatively easy to rally people together, to have them stand up and be counted during tragic, crisis experiences. People will make all kinds of commitments under pressure. However, the majority of them are nowhere to be found the next day when the real hard work needs to be done. Nonetheless, God has a remnant, a church within the church, who remain faithful to do His bidding and who are following in His direction.

CHAPTER 23

The Call at Candlestick Park

DURING THE EARLY 90S AND ON INTO THE 2000S, many new prophetic voices began to emerge who had a strong commitment to seeing the Body of Christ in a particular city and region revitalized. The primary mission was to call the church to repentance and renewal and to re-activate the gifts of the Holy Spirit in order to confront the spiritual and moral decay, which was invading our cities and blanketing our nation.

Two prominent West Coast leaders at that time were Pastor Che Ahn, of Harvest Rock Church in Pasadena, and Lou Engle, an intercessory revivalist, who impacted many churches and college campuses with a spiritual awakening and championed the prayer and worship rallies throughout the United States.

One of the first cities they targeted for this personal and cor-porate call to unification, repentance and intercession was San Francisco at the historic Candlestick Park, which has since been torn down. As they proceeded with the planning, my son, Patrick Kiteley, was contacted to begin forming a team to lead this event, and many of those who initially assisted with the organization and administration were from the University of California, Berkeley, where Patrick held a weekly event for some years known as "Impact." Many San Francisco pastors and churches were personally contacted first and asked to participate in order to try to deal with some of the complaints and offenses of the past. We were aware that too many ministries had come to San Francisco to evangelize and failed to acknowledge the resident pastors already committed to ministering in the city. This resulted in some feelings of being ignored and overlooked. These were the spiritual leaders of the city who had borne the burden and plowed the field in the heat of the day, and they needed to be honored.

This was a formidable task, as some of the local church leaders had a rather lukewarm, wait and see attitude, and others embraced "The Call" in a wholehearted manner. On the day of the event, a number of major national protests were going on in the city of San Francisco, so officials blocked off many of the streets and thoroughfares and closed down some public transit. This can cause total gridlock in the city, especially during tourist season, when San Francisco can host as many as a million visitors a day.

Nevertheless, our numbers spiked to over 40,000 from all over California and from other parts of the nation. The majority of these were serious, sold-out God seekers, who were totally committed to changing the spiritual climate of San Francisco as well as the surrounding regions. Their desire was to see the State of California and the entire nation reclaimed for the Kingdom of God. A few witches, warlocks and Satanists showed up at the gates, but were utterly powerless to function due to the overwhelming presence of God that permeated the whole place.

Candlestick Park was electrified that day with super anointed bands and prophetic messages calling God's people to repentance, and there were long seasons of individual and corporate prayer. There were testimonies of physical, emotional and relational healing that took place. One of the highlights of the day was the testimony of Pastor Javier Ramos, who related the story of how his mother, his siblings and he had literally been abandoned by his father. He candidly shared his feelings of anger and resentment that he had toward him. He also shared that he came to realize that he could not go forward or progress as a Christian if he couldn't forgive his father, whether he asked for it or not. Pastor Javier then gave an altar call, and hundreds of young people came from the bleachers and joined the young people who were already on the playing field for a prayer of repentance. They were ready to let go of any anger or hurt that they felt toward their parents, or in any other relationship that was dysfunctional.

The crowd, instead of diminishing, kept enlarging throughout the day and the Spirit of God was very evident in each speaker, worship band and prayer session. My son, Patrick, and the anointed leadership team kept incorporating all of the participants, seemingly at just the right time, to keep the day moving forward. So, this was not just another routine, large, outdoor Christian concert.

Near the end of the day, the Master of Ceremonies requested that all the San Francisco pastors, ministry directors and non-profit coordinators meet at a designated place at the rear of the park complex. The purpose of this meeting was to allow the suburban leaders to officially meet and greet the urban leaders and ultimately form ongoing ministry partnerships. This session was to help provide manpower, resources and assistance with their outreaches in order to expand and grow their ministries within the city. Later, it was also announced that several thousands of dollars were raised to give to the Mayor of San Francisco to assist with efforts to help the city's homeless.

If you can imagine, I almost missed the entire day, which I had diligently worked on behind the scenes for several months. I was involved in contacting spiritual leaders and ministers, urging them to get their churches involved, as well as contacting neighboring churches they were in fellowship with and asking them to get involved and to financially support this effort if possible. However, four days before "The Call" was to convene, I experienced extreme pain in my lower intestines. Reluctantly, I went to the emergency room, and the doctors immediately hospitalized me. After a battery of tests, the doctor's diagnosis was that I had a twisted bowel that would require surgery as soon as possible. Just after getting this disturbing news, I heard my rather conservative Icelandic wife, Marilyn, loudly praying in the women's restroom and pounding on the wall saying, "Enough is enough! My husband cannot take any more surgeries!" I had already undergone several surgeries, the last instance being a loss of a kidney.

My wife told the Catholic nurse compiling the surgical paperwork that she was expecting a total miracle. The nurse replied that nothing would give her more pleasure than to tear up the surgical orders. Members of our family and pastoral leadership gathered in the hospital to pray a unified prayer of faith and supernatural healing. The doctor decided to order just one more ultrasound before proceeding with the surgery. The doctors and medical staff stated that they miraculously witnessed my intestines untwisting right before their eyes on the screen. I went back to normal, and they canceled the surgery. My wife was able to go back to the nurse and tell her that her desire to tear up the surgical orders had been granted and the miracle had just transpired. I was released the next day, just in time to get ready for "The Call."

The doctor couldn't believe what he had just witnessed and advised me to keep my hospital identification wristband on because he thought it was possible I'd be returning in a couple of days to be operated on, as the intestines often would become twisted again when they were traumatized in that manner. Suffice it to say, I never returned. I've had a number of colonoscopies, and my intestines continue to be normal.

Now this incident clearly reconfirmed to me that there are times as children of God when we experience instant miracles, and they become permanent living testimonies of our human experience. However, it is also true that the majority of miracles take place progressively. During those times, we discover that the greatest manifestation of the anointing is not necessarily to function in all of the gifts of the Spirit, to heal the sick and be a miracle worker, but rather to be able to persevere and endure until the answer fully comes. The biggest lesson I learned is that we have no control whatsoever concerning what or how God chooses to perform His sovereign work, other than to say, "Amen" to His will and His way.

PART IV

Overseas Ministry

As a young lad, I earnestly answered every "Here am I! Send me!" foreign missions call, regardless of the nation or continent. It has been obvious that God seriously took me at my word, and I have had the distinct privilege of ministering in over 45 nations (some of them multiple times) ever since. The overseas missions of Part IV will serve to underscore that the harvest in many nations is ripe, thanks in part to our forbearers, who willingly endured unspeakable persecution, and in some extreme cases, martyrdom, even though they often did not see the fruit of their labors in their lifespan.

May you receive an inspired vision of the unprecedented harvest, which is now ripe and overripe in many nations as you read this section.

CHAPTER 24

VIP Trip to China

IN THE EARLY '80S, I TOOK A TEAM OF ABOUT 25 PEOPLE ON a two-week China missions tour to visit many of the most popular historic sites. China had only been open to the outside world for a couple of years. Fifty percent of the cost of this five-star premium trip was paid for by the Chinese Department of Tourism.

Our missionary leader, Dennis Balcombe, had instructed us to travel light so that we could take as many gift-wrapped Bibles and study guides as possible. The immigration officers immediately detected that we were loaded with some extremely heavy suitcases, which was not the norm for the majority of tourists. These were the days before scanners, so they began opening our bags. We had a photographer traveling with us set up a tripod and start taking pictures of the officers removing our Bibles from the suitcases. I told them through an interpreter that these pictures were going to be sent to U.S. newspapers to inform them of the kind of treatment that U.S. tourists received when traveling in China. I also stated that it would be tremendously embarrassing for us to have no gifts to give to our friends we were going to meet in various cities. After a long discourse, and a lot of silent prayer, God was merciful to us. The head immigration officer, who was by then very frustrated, told his junior officers to put the gift-wrapped

Bibles back in the suitcases, place them all on a truck and take them across the border for us.

We had to rent an extra room at each location just to house the Bibles and study materials. A few of us delivered them at night to Christian homes and drop-off spots throughout the cities we visited. Our Chinese communist guide was very curious as to what we had in that extra room. We told him that no one was permitted to enter at any time without knowing the special code, and we were hoping that before the trip was over that we might be able to let him in on the secret. Our guide on more than one occasion inquired about why I was sleeping in the back of the bus, as I had paid all this money to come on this trip but was not getting out to view the sights. Of course, he knew nothing about the late-night deliveries and how exhausted we were the next day. I told the guide that when the sun was up in China, it was down in the United States and that was one of the reasons that I was so tired. He seemed to act like he understood even though there was a very bewildered look on his face.

After an unforgettable, once-in-a-lifetime, whirlwind trip through major cities and China's attractions, we were airborne again, en route to Tokyo for a brief scheduled stopover at our church, Shinjuku Shalom Church. They had just obtained a new facility, which we were there to dedicate. It was in the heart of Tokyo, just a few blocks away from the busiest train station in the world where three million people passed through every day. After delivering my dedication message, I became extremely dizzy and passed out on the stage. When I came to, a number of Japanese church members were hovering over me. I heard one of them say in broken English, "He has probably been eating too much Asian food and needs a U.S. McDonald's hamburger in order to get back his energy." Meanwhile, a couple of our brothers, Dean Gourley and Darryl Saunders (a former linebacker for the Detroit Lions), were scouting out a few hospitals in the city. They finally settled on an old Catholic hospital where the surgeon could not speak a word of English and had to speak through an American nun who was a nurse there. The surgeon stated that a tumor had burst and ruptured my intestines, resulting in peritonitis throughout my system. He went on to explain that I needed emergency surgery because in his estimation I had less than two hours to live. I was 35 years of age at the time and had two young children. I said goodbye to the two brothers and told them that if I did not make it, I would meet them on the other shore. They prayed for me as the medical personnel began preparing me for surgery.

The next thing I knew, I was in a room in the ICU, and they told me that my wife would be coming in just a few hours. I found out later that God had awakened her in the night and told her to find her passport, which she had not looked at for several months. Of course, she had no idea why He asked her to do that. At four o'clock in the morning, she received a phone call from Japan telling her to come as quickly as possible as I was undergoing emergency surgery.

It was a rather grueling experience because the Japanese old school doctors at that time were not prone to give very much in the way of pain pills because they believed that patients in U.S. hospitals often became junkies. Even though the surgery was successful, after 11 days they could not get my 104-degree fever down, and I was extremely weak, disoriented and depressed with the lack of progress. God woke me up in the night and told me that I had to leave the hospital if I was planning on living. I removed whatever medical equipment was attached to me and got dressed. When my wife woke up, she was terrified and thought I had lost my senses. However, after I explained the situation to her, she agreed that I was right and that we must press forward in faith if we had any chance of making it. We called our missionary and asked him to get enough money to pay off the hospital and purchase two first-class, one-way tickets on Japan Airlines to San Francisco.

The hospital refused to release me at first, but I told them that they could not hold me because I was not a Japanese citizen. I told them that I never remembered signing in to the hospital in the first place.

One of the biggest challenges was that I could not show any sign of weakness when boarding the airplane or they would have requested a medical clearance from the hospital. I remember being in seat 1B with my head turned toward the bulkhead refusing everything they tried to serve me except ice water. I am sure they thought that something was wrong, but were too polite to say anything. When we arrived at the San Francisco Airport and opened the door of the aircraft, a gurney was waiting. An immigration officer told the head steward that they were there for a medical emergency, and the steward stated that there was no one like that on the plane. We identified ourselves and were rushed through the airport out a back door to a waiting ambulance. I got a brief glimpse of my children waving at me; they were greatly relieved because they thought they might never see their father again.

When I got inside the ambulance, the attendant said, "I know you! You are David Kiteley, and I remember you praying for me when I became a Christian and received the baptism of the Holy Spirit."

I said, "That is great, but now I need you to start praying for me." When you invest in someone else's life, God is always faithful to have them or somebody else invest back in you. It is a sure thing, like money in the bank. When I got to Kaiser Hospital in Oakland, they again prepped me for surgery, and this time they left me open so that I could drain from the inside out. I remained at home for a couple of months, but slowly got back on my feet and returned to my normal pastoral duties at the church.

It was a harrowing experience. God clearly spoke to me during that time and said that when you face death head-on, it can never be an enemy that will terrify you again. That was 36 years ago, and by God's grace and mercy I have got a few years left.

Humor in Ministry
HAIRCUTS IN JAPAN

One day my wife and I, along with another pastor couple, arrived in Tokyo after a long, nonstop flight from San Francisco. My mother met us there, announcing that we were already late for a church service.

She suggested that we change in the public, co-ed airport restroom. She stated that in order for us to be well received, the men needed to wear a blue or black suit and the women a long skirt or dress.

When we arrived one hour late to the service, we discovered that everyone there, including the Japanese pastors, were dressed in modern, casual sports attire and were extremely surprised to see us just off the plane, dressed for a wedding. Pastor Violet apologized and said, "Please forgive me." She said that she may have been wrong about the dress code, since it was a Saturday afternoon. She went on to say, however, that in the next few days, we would be in a much more formal conference setting and that long hair on men in the ministry would in no way be accepted. So, in compliance with these rigid rules, we found a barber who spoke very little English. We tried to explain with hand motions that we needed to have our hair cut very short and our sideburns shaved off.

When we finally came out of the barbershop, we looked like two new army recruits who were just going into boot camp. To make matters worse our wives refused to walk on the same side of the street with us or even acknowledge that they knew us. They started laughing uncontrollably, making us feel very self-conscious indeed. The next day, when we arrived at the conference, it was totally evident that we were quite out of fashion. We undoubtedly looked to them like U.S. GIs from a bygone era. All the pastors had meticulous, stylish, modern haircuts, much longer than ours ever were. They were also dressed in very fashionable, modern, western attire.

LESSON LEARNED: Try to inquire in advance about the dress code and hairstyles, especially in a foreign nation, where you have been invited to minister, unless you want to become a spectacle.

CHAPTER 25

China Trip— November 1993

O NE OF THE GREATEST REVIVALS IN CHURCH HISTORY is currently occurring in China where approximately 30,000 people a day are being birthed into the Kingdom of God. History records that in 1949, there were only an estimated three million Christians when the nation came under a brutal communist regime. Many of these Christians were elderly and were at least third and fourth-generation believers. Today, there are well over a hundred million believers, and the vast majority of them are either first or second-generation Christians. Most of them were supernaturally brought to the Lord in the rural agricultural regions through the house church movement, which began with the opening up of China to foreigners in 1979.

Dennis Balcombe, sent out as a missionary from our Oakland church in 1969, had a strong conviction that China was going to open its doors so that Christianity could be preached again. Many prominent ministries thought Dennis was preaching heresy; one even referred to him as "God's fool." But, Dennis kept believing and raised up a church in Hong Kong. Ten years later the miracle of the opening of China began to become a reality, and today he is known as one of the principal founding fathers of the Holy Spirit house church movement, which is continuing to sweep many of the provinces of the nation.

In the last couple of decades, the younger generations have been moving to the cities. There are better educational and career opportunities there because China's economy has rapidly grown over this time to become the second largest in the world. God obviously had a master plan to supernaturally reach this younger generation of Chinese while they were still in the rural regions of the country. Had this not transpired, they would have been totally immersed in the highly competitive and materialistic culture of urban Chinese life. Had they not been touched by the power of the Holy Spirit prior to migrating to the cities, they would have, undoubtedly, not been as receptive to any meaningful Christian involvement. Instead the cities are continuing to be impacted by the Holy Spirit, in ways unprecedented since the days of the early church.

For example, there are over 3,000 known house churches in Shanghai alone. Many of these young, professional, Spirit-filled believers are extremely fervent and have a global vision to train, equip and send missionaries from China all over the world, including the United States. A Chinese passport will allow them legal access into all the predominately Muslim nations without a visa. Their ultimate goal is to evangelize each region and nation down the old "Silk Road," all the way back to the city of Jerusalem. There was obviously a preordained, divine strategy setting in motion a profound visitation of the Holy Spirit upon the Chinese people as a means of producing end-time harvesters.

One of the greatest privileges of my life was to witness the young Chinese Church in action. This was during a prophetic conference trip to eight cities, with a team of six, traveling in Anhui and Hunan provinces in the winter of 1993. Our prophetic team, sponsored by Pastor Dennis, landed in Hefei, Anhui Province. We then drove about 12 hours far into the night in a beat-up, old mini-bus that had definitely seen better days.

The air was bitter cold, the vehicle had no heater and every window in the bus was broken. The roads were treacherous with ice, snow and slush, yet we were determined to not let anything deter us from our solemn mission. We were told that this kind of ministry expedition could only be carried out in the dead of winter. The idea was to camouflage us foreigners with heavy Chinese-style clothing, complete with hats, boots and scarves covering our faces.

An internationally known, prophetic minister heard about our proposed trip and literally begged me to include him on the team. He said it would be a fulfillment of a lifelong dream. He had his secretary phone me a couple of months prior to our scheduled departure date to find out what kind of hotels we were going to be staying at, and we told her to tell him that we were going to be lodging in seven to ten-star hotels in every city where we would be ministering. We said that the number of stars could be easily detected if you just looked up through the holes of the dilapidated thatched roofs on the old, small animal shelters where we would be staying at each location! Suffice it to say, this celebrity prophet soon got a special invitation to take another meeting request in America in a posh hotel. Do you blame him?

We slept on wooden slats covered with bamboo mats and the aroma of barnyard animals. Chickens, ducks and pigs ran around at our feet, and the occasional rat ran up the wall. This provided all the sights, sounds and smells of real rural country living. The main house, where the owner of the property lived, had central heating. This meant they simply would light old, dry grass in the middle of the floor with absolutely no ventilation. This would fill the room with smoke, and we soon became very warm even though we were gasping for breath. The average temperature was between 30–40 degrees Fahrenheit during the day and 10–20 degrees at night.

All of our ministry sessions were outside in the courtyard. One day our missionary, Dennis Balcombe, felt sorry for me as his pastor and had someone go to the city to purchase an electric blanket for me. When we plugged it in, it blew all of the lights in the village compound as well as burned one of my toes. Dennis also brought a portable potty as there were not even any outhouses. A number of the people were so intrigued with the portable potty, that they requested that we give them a demonstration, thinking that this was a new invention that could immediately be imported to the villages, to which we explained that this was not part of the Presbytery Convention ministry.

There were no showers or running water, and we soon discovered that if one did not have a higher purpose for being there, then this was the wrong place unless you were planning to be a martyr. We traveled over 2,000 kilometers and ministered to over 300 ministerial candidates a day in the villages of Anhui and Hunan provinces. At any moment, we could have all been arrested by the Public Security Bureau (PSB), China's police, because it was illegal for foreigners to conduct religious meetings. The property owners were particularly vulnerable and were taking a huge risk allowing us to conduct these prophetic services on their land.

On one occasion, the PSB broke in upon us because one of the officer's wives was there receiving ministry. We left very suddenly, and they chased us on their little motorbikes with their red lights flashing. But we soon left them in the dust. On another occasion, we were stopped by the police in our old, antiquated vehicle because a taillight was burned out, and they wrote a ticket for $30 Chinese, which was approximately $3 U.S. Our missionary, Dennis, was worried that such a payment would be mistaken for a bribe, and that would have set a bad precedent, so even though our bus was full of Bibles and we could've been jailed and deported, he refused to pay the fine.

Our Chinese ministers believed that someone could not be considered a bona fide minister unless they spent some serious time in jail. Our missionary believed this was the best way for all of us to improve our prayer life. Many of the older Chinese spiritual leaders had suffered tremendously including imprisonment in hard labor camps and in some cases even martyrdom, which I greatly respected. However, I let Dennis know that we had no intention whatsoever of going to prison for $3, and if he did not wish to call it a bribe, then call it a gift, and let's get on with our mission.

Each morning in all eight locations, we were abruptly awakened at around 4:30 with a mighty roar of thunderous intercessory prayer, praise and worship. You would think that we had died and woken up in heaven. Most of these indigenous ministerial candidates had either walked or ridden old bicycles 60–70 kilometers on rough dirt roads and, of course, with no maps or GPS or any form of communication. In fact, a number of them testified that God actually told them what village to go to in advance, and they would amazingly arrive right on time even though they had not been given any directions by any other believer or leader.

Seventy percent of the young leaders were women and were just as fervent and dedicated as the men, if not more so. Each day we broke up into three groups and ministered prophetically to 100 candidates through an interpreter. This meant that we ministered to a total of 2,400 candidates in eight days from 6 a.m. to 6 p.m. with hardly any breaks other than a noon meal. The Lord would often give us names like Daniel, Ruth or Esther and they would tell us through the interpreter that those names were the English equivalents of their Chinese names. When the ministerial candidates finally received a word after waiting, sometimes for several hours, in the freezing cold, they would have to leave immediately to go home and make room for the others who were waiting, sometimes all day. There were no chairs; they had to sit on the freezing ground or stand. To them the danger and discomfort of being ministered to in these illegal meetings was more precious than anything that money could buy.

At noon, we had a brief break for some soup with chicken heads and feet and carp fish complete with eyeballs, tails, heads and who knows what else. I was told that they are known to eat rats, which they claim are very delicious and edible because they are domestic grain-fed rats not sewer rats. However, to me a rat is a rat regardless of what qualifying label you may attempt to put on it. I came back with 40 percent of my liver eaten up. I had what the doctor diagnosed as a rare form of hepatitis. They also removed my gall bladder, which was infected at the time. I still have liver disease and take medication daily. I have been asked if I would ever consider going on a trip like that again knowing what I know now about the health issues. My answer is yes, indeed.

There is a cost to birth a revival, yet what kind of price can you put on that kind of a Holy Spirit visitation, anyway? Those services were one of the early catalysts that sparked a revival throughout all of Hunan Province where there are now over ten million believers. Many of these ministerial candidates began to immediately set the prophetic words into operation on their return trips home. They would stop in parks and begin praying for the sick and the mentally ill, and there were confirmed reports of the miracles that transpired. There were also home churches birthed throughout the whole region where these mini-conferences were held.

On the way back to Hefei, we stopped at a four-star hotel in our old beat-up mini-bus. We looked like the Beverly Hillbillies and definitely smelled a whole lot worse, having slept in all our clothes for eight days and gone without showers. When the hotel manager saw us, he immediately informed us that the hotel was completely full. Moses Vegh, one of our senior team ministers, pulled out his gold card, and all of a sudden everything changed. The hotel manager asked us if we wanted to rent the whole top floor. When we got into our rooms, we threw our dirty stinking suitcases into the bathtubs and started scrubbing them down with hotel towels. We showered, went to bed and dreamed that we were home at last.

In the morning, the hotel manager came up to our missionary Dennis and told him in Chinese that we were the dirtiest, filthiest people that had ever been in his hotel during his 25 years of tenure. He then asked, "Where do you people come from anyway?" and said we were all going to be fined for defacing communist government property. Our missionary quite wisely replied, "We did not bring this dirt from home—we got it right here from your province." He went on to tell him, "You cannot expect tourists to come here, if you don't clean it up." If the manager knew where we had really been during the last eight days and what we were doing to advance the Kingdom of God in Anhui and Hunan provinces, I'm sure we would have done some serious time in jail. I am still totally convinced that it would have been entirely worthwhile.

On another China trip with a group of about 30, including my then teenage son, Patrick, our missionary Dennis Balcombe arranged for us to meet with two pastors who had traveled 37 hours on a train. They had come to share their testimonies and receive impartational prayer and a prophetic word of direction and guidance. Their three-day, third-class train trip meant that they would be standing for a great deal of the journey. If they did get a seat, it would be on a hard, archaic wooden bench. These two precious brothers were fugitives from the law and had not been home to see their families for over seven years. They had been in prison and were subject to hard labor and unwarranted persecution for preaching the gospel. They had been released from prison, and Dennis had prearranged for them to travel to Guangzhou, formerly Canton. They were traveling with fake identification papers in order to pass through the inspection stations.

We agreed to meet them at a remote location on White Cloud Mountain rather than having them come into the city where they could have easily been detected, especially being with 30 western foreigners. Upon arrival, these brothers then traveled for the better part of the day from the train tation up the mountain. They had gone ahead of us and prepared a brush arbor place for all of us to meet in the woods. It was raining steadily, and the local amusement park had closed down at the bottom of the mountain. All of their tour buses were grounded. I felt led to commandeer one of these park buses and offered the driver twice his normal day's salary if he would drive us to the top of the mountain. He was more than happy to comply.

The weather was very cloudy, misty and muggy, and the rain kept pelting down. The brothers had left a little marker by the side of the road to indicate where we were to stop. As we crawled out of the bus, we realized that the route to where they were waiting for us literally took us over the side of the mountain. It was a very steep grade with rough terrain, and we had some people in our group who were well up in their 70s and were fairly feeble. The driver insisted that we prepay the whole cost of the arranged fare. He no doubt thought that we could have been some cult group going over the side of the mountain to commit some religious suicidal ritual.

When we got there, we prayed, sang and listened to our brothers' joyful miracle testimonies of divine protection and provision in the midst of what a lot of ministers in the western world would have termed, in days gone by, "The Great Tribulation." We laid hands on them and ministered to them prophetically. They were so appreciative that they were like little children opening their presents on Christmas morning. We could not help but wonder if they were the ones who should have been ministering to us, as we felt so unworthy and humbled to even be in their presence. They had paid such a dear price for their love for Jesus, and they counted themselves privileged to be able to fulfill the Great Commission in their beloved land of China.

This is a strong indictment against some of us in the western church who complain about everything and will even stay home from church because it is either too hot or cold or the pastor is preaching too many convicting sermons. These brothers today represent millions of new believers through-out China. We had the privilege of visiting their ministry in Hangzhou and saw firsthand the powerful work that the Lord had done through them. Everyone wants a revival on their terms, but there is a huge cost to producing an authentic move of God.

On yet another eventful missionary trip, we were asked to stay in an old factory, which was also being used to hold church. The government officials were not able to discover that the believers were meeting there as well. It was a normal request for guest ministry to teach the Word for eight to ten hours in one session, while the people remained open, attentive and seated on the floor, and no one left. In one service in the old factory, approximately 300 people assembled to be taught and to receive the laying on of hands and prayer for the baptism of the Holy Spirit. I was frankly concerned about how we were going to pray for each of them individually considering how long this usually takes in the United States. However, the Holy Spirit showed up in such a phenomenal manner that everyone en masse supernaturally received the gift of the Holy Spirit. After one simple prayer, everyone began to pray in a prayer language and continued to pray in the Spirit for several hours after their initial infilling.

There was a man there who had been diagnosed with fourth stage liver cancer, and he was as yellow as a lemon. We witnessed the Lord peeling that yellow complexion off him. He went to the doctor the next day, and the cancer was completely in remission after this prayer for the Holy Spirit.

It has been my distinct privilege to take all of my children and their mates and the grandchildren to various mission fields that we have served over the last 40+ years. I have made sizeable personal financial contributions in the names of the grandchildren on various continents with the hope that they will begin to hear the call and feel the pulse of global missions. When my daughter, Melinda, was 13 years old, I took her, our associate pastor and his daughter Nicki to Hong Kong and China.

While we were in Hong Kong, Melinda and Nicki attended a youth camp at an old, rustic YMCA grounds outside the city. The food and living conditions proved, at that time, to be very challenging, and could be considered a third world kind of experience. Melinda renewed her relationship with her friend Sharon, Missionary Dennis Balcombe's daughter. Sharon had apparently told her that she was not a real Christian unless she was willing to die as a martyr. These piercing words made a profound impact on Melinda, especially while she and her traveling companion started packing Bibles to take into Mainland China.

Melinda was determined to not let the border officials confiscate any of her Bibles, even though she was only legally permitted to take in one Bible for her own personal use. When Melinda placed her suitcase on the scanner, the border official somehow got distracted, so she began running as quickly as she could through the border inspection area toward China. The PSB began chasing her and yelling for her to stop. She could not help but hear Sharon's words resonating in her ears, "You are not a real Christian if you are not willing to die as a martyr!" So, Melinda kept running and refused to stop, in order to get into China with all of her Bibles. The officers were not able to catch up with her, and they finally let her go. She had created such a disturbance that all of us on the team were also able to get through without being inspected because no one was manning their stations. In China, we were able to witness the tremendous hunger for the Word of God and people who would line up for hours just to receive prophetic direction.

In 2016, this was still the case, as Melinda and her husband, Pastor Javier, had people lining up at all hours of the night in Southern China to receive prophetic ministry. It was a life-changing experience that not only impacted them, but also our grandchildren Joshua and Cristiana.

LESSON LEARNED: We must give an opportunity for the next generation to experience Christianity outside of our comfortable American setting, which often makes people apathetic and complacent. It is vital that they not take their Christian heritage for granted by failing to give it the respect it so justly deserves.

Humor in Ministry
SLIDES FOLLOWING

There's an old amusing quote from the non-existent "reverse" version of the Bible. It says that the early church went everywhere taking pictures, and the Lord confirmed their trip with slides following. I, Moses Vegh and one of his elders traveled extensively in 17 different nations in a 41-day period, taking scores and scores of pictures everywhere we went. When we finally returned home, we took the negatives and got them developed. The result was 2000 slides.

The hope was that everyone in our family and church would get to experience this amazing missionary adventure from which we had just returned. We excitedly set up the projector in the Vegh's living room in Findlay, Ohio. We noticed from the outset that the children in particular were totally disinterested and had to be literally begged to come into the room to view these memorable slides from our world-class tour. Five minutes into the slide show, the crowd started dwindling as everyone filed into the kitchen to make hoagie sandwiches. Ten minutes later, Moses and I were the only ones left in the room, recalling all the behind-the-scenes stories that had occurred on our once-in-a-lifetime trip. We soon began to realize that no one could appreciate these amazing slides unless they could capture firsthand the sights, the sounds and the smells that brought them all to life. I put all the slides in a box several decades ago, and I have never brought them out since.

My exhortation now is: to anyone who desires to have a missionary experience, sign up for a short-term trip, rather than attempt to see them through someone else's lenses.

CHAPTER 26

The Philippines

WE ARE CREATURES OF HABIT AND WE LIKE OUR LITTLE rituals. We are comfortable with our normal routines. The older we get, the more we have to resist the urge to play it safe. Otherwise you end up becoming very predictable and unwilling to take a risk. We sit in our armchair quarterback seats warning the passionate Peters who are willing to get out of the boat and walk on water, to "Look out for the waves!" We become masters at calculating the length and height and breadth of the water. It is noteworthy that one rarely receives any encouragement from the shallow boat crew, most of whom have yet to navigate the land, let alone walk on water.

I have attended numerous ministerial conferences over the years that have given an abundance of information concerning all the cautions, safeguards and considerations that need to be understood if you are going to make any meaningful progress in the Kingdom of God. However, in the final analysis you feel drained of every bit of faith you possessed prior to going to these conferences. As a result, you become content to stay in your secure fortress and never risk venturing out beyond established limits.

Fortunately, we serve a sovereign God, and much of the good we do in advancing the Kingdom is done unintentionally when we are unaware of what the long-term effects of our actions are going to be. Two of these phenomenal incidents transpired on missions trips to the Philippines. We just stumbled onto these miracles without any prior planning.

The first one was in 1988 near the University of Makati, Philippines. Moses Vegh and I had been ministering propheti- cally in a church, which at that time had about 100 people, and which is now in excess of 50,000, and has many other exten- sion ministries throughout the nation and the world. While we were driving through that region, we spotted an area that had been blocked off. We later found out the area held a crowd of about 68,000 people who were holding a large protest rally against the Marcos regime.

The streets were all sealed off, and there was a heavy police and military presence to maintain crowd control and order. I told our driver to proceed toward the blocked area, which was directly behind the speakers' stage. When we arrived at the barricade, the officer signaled to us to make a U-turn and exit out of the area. At that moment, Moses Vegh pulled out his of- ficial looking ambassador card with the name of his ministry. The officer apologized, saluted us and ordered that the barri- cades be pulled back. We were directed to park right behind the speakers' stage.

My son, who was a teenager at the time, asked, "Dad, now what are we going to do?" I told him and Moses that God must have brought us there for a purpose, and we must not lose this opportunity.

So, I got out of the car and proceeded up the stairs to the speakers' stage. I felt compelled by the Holy Spirit to request the emcee give me a couple of minutes to address the crowd. He asked me who I was, and I told him I was a visiting minister from America. Within a couple of minutes, I was requesting that the crowd lift their hands to the God of the Philippines and repent and pray for reconciliation and healing for their nation, and then proceeded to lead them in a brief prayer for salvation. They were extremely responsive, and it appeared that this had been a divine setup in order to speak peace and redemption over the city and the university students.

By that time, my son and Moses were calling for me to come down from the stage right away as a security officer had discovered that I was not scheduled to address the crowd. We made a quick exit, and on the way out a woman asked me to take her baby home with me to America to my wife. I declined politely, we got in the car and they opened the barricades. We thanked God that He had given us opportunity to declare His name in the midst of those rallying protestors. It was definitely a God-appointed event, for which Moses Vegh's ambassador card came in handy.

The second God-ordained event occurred in the late '80s when we took a team to minister on the island of Mindanao in the Philippines. This island has long been known as a place where foreigners are taken hostage for ransom. Nonetheless, several Shiloh Christian churches were either adopted or established on that island. We were going there to conduct a conference and training session for leaders. We arrived at a small airport at Pagadian, and, without any prior notice, I was ushered into the presence of a waiting Police Chief with an armed guard holding an AK-47 in the back of the vehicle.

I told him that I would not be going anywhere without my teenage son, and they went and brought him to the jeep. Patrick was quite concerned that we were getting into some major trouble. There were also a number of vehicles waiting there for the rest of the team. The police had assigned personal bodyguards for each of them.

I was asked to pick up the phone in the vehicle and talk to the governor who welcomed us to the region and stated that he heard that I was a prophet and wanted me to come and minister to his staff and family. He stated that he had arranged a police escort for our team and was looking forward to meeting us. When we arrived at the governor's home, we asked all of their staff to put out their cigars. We then led them in the sinner's prayer and proceeded to give them prophetic words.

We went to the family and prayed for some members who believed God had ordered this entire visit. The governor then asked me to tell him how he could assist us with our ministry in the regions, and we told him about our need for a building to conduct meetings. He then offered to give us the lower floor of the governor's house, free of charge, to open a church.

Nothing of significance is ever accomplished until you are willing to be strong and courageous, step out on the water, break with your normal routine and move beyond the established limits.

Humor in Ministry

UNHOLY WATER

It is a rare privilege to be invited to stay in the home of a well-known Christian statesman and his family, particularly in another nation where the culture is entirely different than what we are used to. The home we were invited to stay in was the home of the general secretary of one of the oldest and largest Pentecostal denominations in Indonesia. Things were going along remarkably well, and we were seemingly positively interacting with everyone, including the children. It appeared that they were genuinely excited to have us staying with them in their home, despite the fact that the kids were crowded out of their bedrooms and sleeping on the floor. Little did we know that this whole atmosphere of grace and goodwill was in the process of changing very rapidly.

One night a member of our ministry team discovered a large 50-gallon drum and removed the lid. To his delight it was full of cool, clear, clean water. Without giving it any thought, he proceeded to undress and climb into this large water tank with his soap, shampoo and shaving cream. As this old farmer would put it, he was as content as a cow eating molasses. When he got out of this cool, clear, clean water, it was all grey and murky and had greatly lost its original refreshing appeal. Little did he realize that he had just totally contaminated the family's two-week supply of drinking water. It was now barely usable to wash clothes in and would more than likely need to be dumped.

All of a sudden, we were reduced from most favored houseguest status to unwanted, ignorant U.S. missionaries who had overstayed their welcome. After apologizing profusely and offering to pay for a special water delivery to come the next day, things began to somewhat improve.

LESSON LEARNED: When traveling overseas, it's probably much better to stay at an international hotel where, at least, you understand the culture, rather than becoming instantaneously unpopular by contaminating your host's water supply.

CHAPTER 27

Vietnam

ONE OF THE QUESTIONS THE U.S. IMMIGRATION officer asked me prior to my becoming a U.S. citizen in 2007 was, "Why did you list Vietnam as one of the nations that you visited in January 1973 as a green card holder?"

Jokingly I told him, "I had to pay my fare, unlike a number of friends I work with who were drafted and got a free ride." This lighthearted banter caused him to be extremely eager to hear my story concerning Vietnam. I related how I had traveled there as an ordained minister/missionary to be a support system for and to encourage 20 other American missionaries. They had purposed in their heart to live there and even die there if necessary because they said it was "the land of their calling." This is where the story ended with the immigration officer.

The rest of the story was that two other ministers and I had been invited to stay in a large home with some evangelical missionaries. We had been asked to hold a mini-conference on the Holy Spirit during which we were able to lead them into the baptism of the Holy Spirit.

During the next four days, we had long sessions of intercession for the nation as well as in-depth discussions on the operation of the nine gifts of the Spirit[11] and the five-fold ascension gifts.[12] I never will forget the level of hunger and the joyful expression that these missionaries manifested. They stated over and over again how honored they were to minister in Saigon at that time in history.

A peace treaty had been signed the same month that we went there to be missionaries in 1973, although the war would continue to wage on until April of 1975. In Vietnam, 58,220 military servicemen and women died, and countless warriors were wounded permanently during this horrible conflict. While we were there, the skies would often light up at night, and we would hear gunfire going off in the distance.

The missionaries told us that there was growing hostility between the people in South Vietnam and the U.S. because they were beginning to withdraw so many troops from the nation. They felt they were being abandoned and soon could be taken over by the Viet Cong. We were told about isolated incidents of those who received a haircut in the day and then had their throats slit in the night by the same person. The U.S. State Department was urging the missionaries to leave, and they told us they would rather be there in the will of God, than be out of His will and back in the comforts and safe haven of the U.S.

To me, this was extremely challenging, and I realized at that very moment that they were ministering a whole lot more to us than we could ever minister to them. Later we heard reports

---

11. 1 Corinthians 12:8–10 provides: "For to one is given the word of wisdom through the Spirit, and to another the word of knowledge according to the same Spirit; to another faith by the same Spirit, and to another, gifts of healing by the one Spirit, and to another the effecting of miracles, and to another prophecy, and to another the distinguishing of spirits, to another various kinds of tongues, and to another the interpretation of tongues." (New American Standard Bible.)

12. Ephesians 4:11–12 provides: "And He gave some as apostles, and some as prophets, and some as evangelists, and some as pastors and teachers, for the equipping of the saints for the work of service, to the building up of the body of Christ;" (NASB)

on the Associated Press wires that some of the missionaries we met with ended up being martyrs for the Lord.

Everyone loves the ruling and reigning message, which involves popular success and prosperity teaching and the message that promises personal promotion. However, Jesus said if you want to rule and reign with me, you will have to suffer with me. This involves taking up your cross daily and denying yourself for the Kingdom's sake. This is one of the deepest fellowships that a true believer can experience with the Lord. Yet, I do not know how many people will want to sign up for this assignment. It is a level of Christianity that many of us in the modern western world would never choose or even consider. The truth, however, is that it is possible to actually lose your life without physically dying by giving it up for a cause that has no eternal value.

Humor in Ministry
PURCHASING SOUVENIRS OVERSEAS

During a 41-day whirlwind excursion around the world, I came across some unusual souvenirs bargains, which I was sure my wife would love and would be able to find room in our home for. I bought extra suitcases and paid additional fees for exceeding the maximum weight limit on the airplanes. It became increasingly difficult to drag these little trophies in and out of hotels and on and off buses. When I finally got my luggage home, my wife asked me to take the extra suitcases out to the garage so that she could sort through them and make sure I hadn't picked up some exotic bugs along the way. At this point, my wife took out a couple of items, mainly because I insisted on keeping them. She then packed up the rest to be taken to the thrift store or flea market.

I discovered later that all of these international souvenirs can be purchased at the local Cost Plus store where there is more variety, better quality and they are half price!

LESSON LEARNED: Travel light and give your wife the money to purchase what she wants locally, and everyone will be happier and less exhausted.

CHAPTER 28

Miracles in Dacca, Bangladesh

MOST OF THE VITAL LESSONS CONCERNING THE FAITH WALK are learned while we are in the middle of perplexing crises situations and have little or no understanding, whatsoever, about what is transpiring. God rarely chooses to tell us anything in advance—we would probably never even begin the journey in the first place, or we would make every effort to fit it into our scheduled itinerary. Meanwhile, we could miss out on all the supernatural surprises God has planned for us. In Exodus 3, we find Moses in the middle of his uneventful daily routine when he stumbles upon the burning bush on Mount Horeb.

There was no flashing neon sign or prior angelic announcement that stated that he was about to enter the Mount of God. This divine encounter altered the whole focus, direction and destiny of his life from that time onward. He was being re-commissioned to fulfill his initial calling, which had eluded him for decades. It has been aptly stated that most of the long-term productive things that we do for the Lord in our lives we usually do by accident. There is perhaps no better illustration of this than the missionary trip that Moses Vegh, his elder and I made to Dacca, Bangladesh, in 1973.

The following includes excerpts taken by permission from the late Moses Vegh's book, *The Chronicles of Moses*.

While ministering in Bangkok, Thailand, we received a confirmation to fly on to Dacca, Bangladesh where we were scheduled to speak at a pastors' conference. Early in the morning, our plane descended over the Bay of Bengal, and Moses shared with me that what we were viewing from the aircraft was the very picture that he had received in a vision years before. The vision had shown him dugout canoes, old paddleboats, steamers and a great throng of people on the shores. He stated that he was so happy that we were able to be there together to fulfill this prophetic vision that God had given him decades before.

When we arrived in Dacca airport, we were made aware that there were only two flights out each week from that airport. Soon we were in a crowd of thousands of people and were herded toward a 1932 Peugeot taxi. The driver was barefoot and dressed in what appeared to be a bed sheet. He tied our bags on the top of the car, which had no air conditioning, and the temperature was at least 110 degrees. We drove through masses of people, buses, sheep, goats and donkeys, until we finally reached our destination about 30 minutes away from the airport. We pulled up to the conference compound of the major Pentecostal denomination where we were scheduled to speak. The presiding officer at the gate told us that the conference had been cancelled, and he did not even allow us to come in to get a drink of water and freshen up.

He offered no explanation other than we were there on the wrong date. Later on, we found out that the organization sponsoring the event had not embraced the Charismatic Renewal. The director had heard that we were Charismatics, so he cancelled the conference even though he had known Moses Vegh for several years. We had traveled halfway around the world, and there we stood, totally frustrated to say the least. We were wondering why God had allowed us to come to Dacca only to have the door slammed in our faces. We got back into the stifling heat of the old Peugeot and backed down a long alley into the main stream of traffic. There in the middle of the heavy traffic, one of our tires blew out. The driver attempted to jack up the car, but he did not have the proper handle, so he was turning the greasy screw jack with his bare hands.

We could not help but notice that the spare tire was in almost as bad shape as the tire he was replacing. Finally, we joined hands and cried out to God, rebuking the devil that was attempting to rob us of this awesome opportunity to reach many in this war-torn nation. We went back over to the main gate and shook it again. The same leader who had refused us entry came out, and we asked him if God was doing anything that he knew of in the city besides what was going on in their compound. He responded, "Yes, I know whom you should contact," and, seeing our frustration, he finally opened the gate and led us to a phone. He told us to call a certain Swedish Baptist brother who was in charge of a large United Nations distribution office. His name was Bengt Sundberg. When he answered the phone, Sundberg assured us that he would be there in a few minutes to help us and was apologetic for the fact that we were in such a predicament.

He arrived in a new white 1972 Land Rover with air conditioning. We asked him jokingly if he would allow us to just stay in his vehicle for three days until we could catch the next flight out of Dacca. He said, "No, brothers, you are my guests, and you will come to my house." He happened to live next door to the Prime Minister, Sheik Nujibar. We explained in detail how we had been scheduled to be in Dacca for a pastors' conference, but it had been cancelled without notice because we were Charismatics. Now we had all this time on our hands that we could have utilized in other nations where we were gladly accepted.

After we fellowshipped a while and had a meal together, Sundberg said to us, "I know exactly where you are supposed to be." By then it was around noon, and we got in his vehicle. He drove us through a number of desolate areas in the city until we finally arrived at the Holy Cross Convent and girls' high school. High walls surrounded this large compound where a number of children were housed for school, as well as the orphanage. We knocked at the main iron gate, and a young boy opened it. When he saw us standing there, he immediately began to shout, "They are here! They are here!" We looked around bewildered wondering whom he was talking about. He immediately ushered us into the main courtyard, and we saw Sister Margaret come running toward us out of her office. She had her hands in the air and was praying in her heavenly language. She later told us that, just three weeks before, she had been in San Francisco attending a Catholic Charismatic Conference and had received the baptism of the Holy Spirit. She began weeping as she told us that a prophet at the meeting had told her not to fear, that God was going to send a wonderful blessing to her compound in Dacca. He told her that the Lord had already ordered some men who would appear at her gate when she returned. When they arrived, she was to shut down all of the activities and call the staff, leaders and guests into the main chapel. They would then receive the impartation that these men would bring to them from the Word of God, as well as the laying on of hands to receive the Holy Spirit.

Sister Margaret was more than ready. She had already phoned the Mother Superior, and all the nuns and priests from all the parishes in the region, as well as our Baptist brother, Bengt Sundberg, and told them to be there for this outpouring of the Spirit. It was much like the occasion of Acts 10 when the Spirit was poured upon the household of Cornelius. Moses told them about the vision that he had decades before of the Lord calling him to go to Dacca to minister. After a long season of ministry from the Word and prayer and worship, we began to lay hands on all of those present. They began speaking in tongues, and we gave words of prophecy to numbers of them. There was a Seventh Day Adventist pastor, as well as priests, nuns and our Baptist brother, all lying out on the floor because they had been greatly impacted by the Holy Spirit.

Sister Margaret shared with us again after the meeting that she had been in San Francisco three weeks before when she received the prophetic word concerning men who would be showing up at her gate. We calculated that she had left San Francisco the same day that we had left from the same airport to start our journey around the world. We had been traveling for three weeks in several different countries before we arrived in Dacca. She prevailed upon us to minister extensively to every one of her team members and pleaded with us to send another ministry team to them as soon as possible.

A couple of years later, while I was ministering in southern India at a large conference, one of the main leaders who was hosting me told me about how the move of the Holy Spirit was sovereignly brought to Bombay (now known as Mumbai). He said that three angels had come from America and arrived at the door of the Holy Cross Convent in Dacca, Bangladesh, and that a Holy Ghost revival broke out there. He went on to say that the nuns then brought the Holy Spirit message to the convents in Mumbai. The man said that, at that time, there were only a couple of Spirit-filled ministries functioning in the Charismatic gifts of the Spirit in that whole city of several million people. He said, "Now there are over 1,100 Spirit-filled ministries, and the revival is spreading throughout the whole region."

In retrospect, I am glad that we did not know that our conference had been cancelled at the Pentecostal compound. I am glad that we did not know in advance that we were going to be rerouted to a Catholic convent because, quite honestly, up until that time I would have never even considered going to minister in a Catholic convent in the United States, let alone travel halfway around the world to do so. Also, it would have never been my choice to go to Dacca.

Humor in Ministry

NUNS IN THE ELEVATOR

In 1973, my wife and I attended a conference in Pittsburgh, Pennsylvania at Duquesne University, during which time our son, Patrick, was only six weeks old. This was near the beginning of the Charismatic Movement, which powerfully impacted the historical churches such as the Catholic, Lutheran and Episcopal churches, as well as several other denominations who were touched by the Holy Spirit in an unprecedented manner. Unfortunately, this was often generally frowned upon at that time by more established Pentecostals. They felt these people should join their denomination, as they were the "original gatekeepers" when it came to people being filled with the Spirit.

I had been told, prior to going to the conference, that many of the Catholic nuns were much more demonstrative than many other groups that had traditionally spoken in tongues and functioned in the nine gifts of the Holy Spirit found in 1 Corinthians 12. We were staying in a room on the upper floor of one of the university's residential buildings. I went down to the cafeteria on the first floor to warm the formula for our new baby. When I entered the elevator to return to our room, I was literally swarmed with a number of Catholic nuns laying hands on me, shaking me and speaking in tongues at the top of their lungs. They no doubt believed that I was a completely dried out, empty soul that needed to be filled with the Spirit and to begin speaking in tongues.

I became aware that the floor we were staying on had come and gone. The nuns had rigged the elevator so that it would keep going up and down from top to bottom and not stop to let anyone on or off. The elevator had made many trips up and down before they finally discovered that I too possessed this gift. They obviously could not hear me speaking in tongues, because they were yelling so loud. They finally apologized and let me out of the elevator. I explained to them that, although I enjoyed this full-on prayer meeting, I needed to get back with some warm milk for our new six-week-old baby.

LESSON LEARNED: Never get into an elevator crowded with Charismatic nuns unless you are ready to be detained for an extended period of time.

CHAPTER 29

New Zealand Christmas 1972

HISTORICAL RECORDS INDICATE THAT THE APOSTLE Paul first went to the city of Corinth in A.D. 51. The city had a worldwide reputation for idolatry, immorality and perversion. It was also known for its thievery, extortion and even murder. Corinth was a thriving seaport with high-powered salesmen and influential, elegant speakers with superb showmanship. Paul had been up on Mars Hill, which is near where the Acropolis still stands in Athens today, just before arriving at Corinth.

At Mars Hill, Paul participated in a daily eight to ten-hour intellectual, philosophical debate. He attempted to answer questions concerning eternity and the hereafter, as well as the mystery that they referred to as the "unknown god." They primarily believed in the Epicurean philosophy of, "Let's all eat, drink, and be merry and live it up because tomorrow we are all going to die anyway." The Apostle Paul learned a very painful lesson at Mars Hill in Athens. This was the only place in all of his extensive missionary journeys where he never planted a church or had one reported convert.

When Paul came to Corinth, he came to them with a great deal of physical weakness, fear and trembling (1 Corinthians

2). He made it clear that the power in his words had nothing to do with man's wisdom, with his speaking abilities or with his charismatic presentation. Instead, the power of his words came from the power of the sovereign God. This type of power could never be produced by human instrumentality.

This important truth became a reality on the first leg of Moses Vegh's and my 41-day missionary tour around the world. Scheduled to minister in 17 nations, we left San Francisco on Christmas night, 1972, bound for Auckland, New Zealand. With fewer than a dozen passengers on a plane that can hold up to 300, there were eight flight attendants on board, so we were lavishly and personally taken care of. The late Moses Vegh, with whom I've traveled to over 35 countries, stayed up all night witnessing and praying for all the flight attendants on the plane and completely lost his voice. All he could do was grunt and shake his head like the Priest Zacharias before his son, John the Baptist, was born.[13] I tried to get some sleep and when I woke up, there was a severe cramp in my leg, which I had never had before or have had since. I was limping like Jacob when the angel put his thigh out during a wrestling match.[14] It was extremely painful, and I felt like a disabled man. After arriving in Auckland, we travelled to our first scheduled meeting, which was at a campground about 35 miles north of the city. They had erected a large tent to accommodate the crowd and had a sign announcing that this was to be a miracle meeting with guests from America who had healing and prophetic gifts. It was a rather humbling experience to begin our first ministry meeting on our scheduled 17-nation missionary tour in such a handicapped manner. When the pastor introduced us, Moses assisted me as I hobbled up to the stage, and I introduced him like a ventriloquist as he nodded his head in agreement.

At that moment, the 1 Corinthians narrative began to take on an expanded meaning as one of us could not talk and the other

---

13. Luke 1.

14. Genesis 32.

one could not walk. And yes, we were being introduced as healers from America! We realized that at that very moment our strength was not going to be vindicated through our ability to function with our spiritual giftings, but rather through the presence of the Holy Spirit compensating for our disabilities as we acknowledged our weaknesses. Scriptures such as "Let the weak say I'm strong,"[15] and "His strength is made perfect in our weakness,"[16] all of a sudden became a new reality. The result was that we witnessed more extraordinary miracles and life-changing results in those Auckland meetings than in many of the nations we went on to minister in on that trip. This is primarily because the people were so receptive to how honest and vulnerable we were about our human weaknesses. This taught me a lifelong lesson: the power was not in our presentation, but rather in releasing His grace into every situation.

---

15. Joel 3:10.

16. 2 Corinthians 12:9.

CHAPTER 30

Soviet Union and Ukraine

IN THE MID-'80S, WE BEGAN WORKING EXTENSIVELY with Bob Weiner, President of Maranatha Ministries. This university campus ministry was responsible for establishing churches all over the U.S. and in many foreign nations.

These young leaders were totally, 100 percent, sold out, and many of them were academically in the top five percentile in their colleges. The goal was to send them back to their cities and nations so that they could become major leaders within the Body of Christ and within the secular world.

In the '80s we co-sponsored a missions trip to the former Soviet Union. More than 1,000 young people from all 11 time zones across Russia attended our event. At that time, the Russian economy was in such shambles that they could fly round trip from anywhere in the nation to Moscow for $3 U.S., and they were also able to stay for five days at the Olympic Izmailovo Hotel for $2/day, which included food and lodging.

This was a brief window of opportunity, and we struck while the iron was hot. We traveled from there to Kiev, and God sovereignly allowed us to rent the largest downtown auditorium for $50 U.S. We met a Spirit-filled man on the street, a pastor who was willing to be our interpreter. We pointed to 7:00 p.m. on our watches and then pointed to the auditorium in order to advertise the meeting. When we opened the doors, thousands of people were waiting to get in. After the Word was preached, an altar call was given, and almost everyone raised their hands for salvation. We asked anyone who wanted to receive the Holy Spirit, which we had briefly taught about, to come forward to the large platform, and hundreds came.

Our whole team began praying, and all kinds of miracles took place among the people who had recently been released from communism, and knew little or nothing about what we were presenting.

Bishop Bart Pierce was able to plant a church in Ukraine in the city where we were ministering, as a result of that missions effort.

Bob Weiner recently sent my wife and me an email which stated, "Both you and your mother have blessed the world and had a major impact on the former Soviet Union, and today there are a half million people who were directly affected as result of your ministry in Moscow."

That is amazing considering the fact that it was about 30 years ago and the seed sown back then is still bearing fruit!

CHAPTER 31

Romania Story

I N THE LATE SPRING OF 1990, AN APOSTOLIC LEADER, who was a superintendent of a Pentecostal movement in Romania, came to our church in Oakland. He presented a passionate "Macedonian call,"[17] a desperate plea for immediate help for his nation. He tearfully related how Romania had an enormous spiritual vacuum and that the harvest was ripe and overripe. He stated that it was mandatory that the church worldwide take immediate action. Little did we know how accurate this statement would prove to be. We assembled a team of 30 people from various parts of the U.S.; the team was made up of pastors, musicians and mission-minded evangelists as well as humanitarian mercy workers. We were scheduled to leave near the beginning of July in 1990. This trip will be forever etched in all of our memories.

Our story begins with Nicolae Ceausescu, the former president of Romania, who was building a new palace, which he never occupied due to his assassination on December 25 of 1989. The palace was said to contain 1000 rooms at the cost of $2 billion U.S. in 1990. To make room for it, 16 churches, 3 monasteries, 2 synagogues and more than 299 homes had to be destroyed. Ceausescu had more than 50 castles decorated

---

17. "Macedonian call" refers to a God-given vision that directed the route Paul took on his second missionary journey (Acts 15:39—18:22).

with gold, connected by 28 miles of underground tunnels. Thousands of guards and servants served the Ceausescu domain. All this luxury was obtained by exporting most of Romania's production. Romanian TV had featured the palace of Ceausescu. One gate weighing 1100 pounds was made of gold and encrusted jewels, as were the candelabras and fixtures in the bathroom. Meanwhile the populace starved, which was never publicly exposed until after his death.

The new leader of Romania was also part of the Communist Party, but was allowing, at least for the present, a considerable amount of freedom to practice and spread Christianity. Many of the Christians were very suspicious and concerned about the longevity of this freedom. The communists had developed an archaic bureaucracy based on fear, intimidation and suspicion. Everyone was involved in checking and re-checking everyone else. No one trusted anybody.

The average wait at the border to get into Romania was 8 to12 hours. One lady had been in line for five hours (she was then the second car). People were extremely angry with us because we went to the head of the line since we had Red Cross signs on our vehicles. Even with that, it took us two hours to get processed. The cost for going through all these borders would normally have been $60/person, and we had 30 in our group. This was all waived due to letters received from the Red Cross and United Nations. Those letters also saved the group from $50-$60/day in the Romanian hotels. There were two prices, one for the Romanians at $2-$3, and one for the western tourists at $50-$60/night. But they waived all of those expenses.

The communist government paid for all of our hotels. They gave us 500 liters of unleaded gas, which was very scarce in Romania. In fact, one guy bought some gas from us for $22/liter, which we had purchased for only $0.07/liter.

There was a total lack of authority in the nation. No one knew who was really in charge. One sign on the side of a building in Timisoara read, "No Future." This was true unless God intervened. We believed He would answer the cry of the people in the nation.

The hotels were all riddled with bullet holes and a lot of the windows were cracked. The first night in the hotel in Santa Maria, a woman came into our room in the middle of the night and wanted to sleep on our extra couch. She was screaming and yelling; she appeared to be totally overcome with fear and trauma. That was our first introduction to the "great adventure" in Romania.

Two men, Darryl and Louie, drove two 7-ton trucks and went in through another route carrying hospital beds, a large generator which would operate a whole intensive care unit, syringes and needles and an assortment of medicines to be taken to the hospital in Cebu.

We met a pastor in Aradia who oversaw 146 churches with a total membership of 90,000. We had a conference in one of his churches with some medical doctors. The doctors told us of the grave needs in the hospitals, and we gave them about 18,000 aspirins, Band-Aids, needles and syringes. In the city, we met the chief medical doctor, who oversaw 400 doctors. He told us his salary was $57/month.

Before we made the trip, we were able to get a list of needs, which we presented to various medical foundations in the United States in order for them to send relief. We took in the equivalent of about $250,000 U.S. of medical supplies in the trucks, which we rented.

There were hundreds of children in the hospitals infected by the AIDS virus because of unsterilized needles and syringes. Up until Ceausescu's murder, the Romanian government would not admit they had any such problems.

We were particularly concerned about the 100,000 children who had been totally dehumanized in the government orphanages we visited. They were treated worse than caged animals would be treated in the United States. Under Nicolae

Ceausescu both abortions and contraception were forbidden. He believed that population growth would lead to economic growth. He banned abortion except in cases in which the mother was over 40 years old or already had four children. People were taxed for being childless. The increase in the number of births resulted in many children being abandoned in orphanages, where perfectly healthy children were placed along with people with disabilities and mental illness. Physical and sexual abuse of the children was reported to be very common. The orphanages lacked medicines and washing facilities, and the children were often tied to their beds or dangerously restrained in their own clothing. Many children died of minor illnesses or injuries that were never attended to. Other children just simply starved to death. There was an epidemic of HIV and AIDS due to unsterilized instruments.

Many parents, sadly, put their children there simply because they could not afford such a large family. They hoped to pick them up at the age of 12 or 13 years old, but were often unable to do so because the children did not relate to their parents anymore and would rather run away or go to another home.[18]

Many of the people who were saved in our Romanian stadium meetings were part of a new breed who were freed from the bondage of the Pentecostal movement, which was at that time extremely pharisaical, to say the least. Romanian church leaders informed us that we were not to clap our hands, dance or pray for the sick. Church members were not permitted to wear rings, wedding bands or lipstick. The men and women were separated from each other in the churches. They would not baptize people unless they had attended there and gone through classes for six months.

---

18. After returning from the church I teamed up with, some members of the Rotary Club and I did a number of speaking engagements in all kinds of unusual places and collected several thousands of dollars for orphanages.

There was an extremely prideful attitude among these leaders. For example, in one city a pediatrician and her daughter gave their hearts to the Lord in a soccer stadium. We tried to introduce her to the pastor in that city, but he would not speak to her because of the jewelry and makeup she was wearing. He said she was a harlot. That was with a lady who had been saved just five minutes. The only hope for the future was to start a whole new ministry outside of the established church.

It is so painful to see the church leadership of Romania refuse to come and lay hands on one of their own people. They stood back with a look of arrogance. They were so caught up in nonessential, legalistic issues. Their empty, vain traditions had destroyed the very life of Christ. For example, a man came to a baptismal service in a large stadium on the last day we were there. It was 115 degrees. This individual had been waiting for 20 years to be baptized, but they would not baptize him because there was no Pentecostal church in the town where he resided. He had to wait until there was a pastor of his denomination there to be baptized.

Several groups traveled to Romania planning to minister, but had no contacts whatsoever. This happened, in part, because of people like the pastor who visited our church and pleaded for people to help. Also, it was a novelty to go into Romania at that time. We soon became aware that unless solid relationships were built, all spectacular, superficial ministry would have no longevity. We were glad that a solid, balanced New Testament church was established in the city of Oradea, where about 100 university students were meeting at that time. It took just $100/month to support a pastor and his family in 1990.

On Sunday mornings, we saw hundreds of people walking, singing and going to churches. We spent our first Sunday morning in a church in Baia Mare, where 1,500 people packed into a church that seated 750. There appeared to be more people standing outside the church than inside.

People responded to the message though, and although we could not get near them individually, we prayed en masse. We also invited them to go to a local church that evening if they wanted more prayer.

That afternoon, we went to a soccer stadium. The response to the music and Word was so overwhelming that we could not handle the crowds. About 500 people swarmed down upon us to be prayed for. We touched as many as we could, and they expressed through interpreters that they just received the Lord, or that they were coming to pray for their whole house to receive the Lord. They requested prayer for deliverance from various habits.

The Romanian people were very intense, and there was a deep hurt and wounding that had taken place after 41 years of oppression. Whenever they got near to the presence of God, they cried out with great intensity. They usually put their hands over their eyes when they did it.

That evening, 800 people showed up at the local church for prayer. This amazed the Romanian leaders, who expected maybe 100 people to show up.

When we arrived in the next city, our host pastor thought that, since there was a Romanian soccer game on that day, perhaps our open-air meeting would not materialize. So, he suggested that we just rest. The whole trip was completely disorganized, unplanned, impromptu, and in most nations, it would have been a complete fizzle. However, in Romania the hunger was so great that you didn't have to go anywhere to have a meeting.

While we were waiting to sort out this round of confusion, a couple of us began talking to an engineer in the hotel lobby. He was paid $27/month. We led him in the sinner's prayer, and he began crying out to God. I looked up and people in the other seats in the lobby all began crying and wanted us to come over and pray for them too. It was obvious that we didn't need to concern ourselves with any schedule, just make ourselves available anywhere. The pastor in that town came two hours later and said, "The people are still waiting in the park for you, why haven't you come?"

News reporters traveled with us. Of the 1100 newspapers in Romania at that time, 1080 were communist and 20 were free news. One of the reporters got saved, baptized and became our interpreter.

The last day before we left Romania, his newspaper put on a banquet for all of us. We met the owners of the newspaper, who were very receptive. They said if we would send them articles, they would give us one full page of the newspaper every week to talk about Christianity. They also stated that one of their greatest problems was that the only press they could print on was owned by communists and was an 1800s model. They wanted us to get in touch with a firm in America or Western Europe so they could buy their own press and be unrestricted.

All their printing equipment dated back to the 1800s and was unbelievably archaic. They had to print all their own textbooks on it. They could not get any outside books from anywhere. The head printer, when we asked what we could do for this nation, said, "Why don't you send us another thousand miners from America who can beat on us for the next five years, and we will supply the clubs. Our people are so stupid; we have taken all of this hands down. And I don't think we've learned our lesson yet."

I quoted him in a message I delivered in a stadium the final Sunday. The communist reporter who was there misinterpreted what I said. She thought I said I was going to bring a thousand miners from the U.S. to beat them up. She was quite irate and thought I was perhaps going to start a new revolution among the common people. We cleared the whole matter up very quickly and talked about the need for accurate interpretation. She not only apologized profusely and corrected the whole matter publicly, but everyone including me got a good laugh out of the whole matter.

The president of the university spoke to us about the vacuum that had been created in the country and the need for a spiritual revolution. He said it was more important than medicine, modern technology or economic redevelopment. He asked if we would consider setting up a "School of Religion" in the university, training students in the Bible exclusively, with the goal of them becoming spiritual leaders in the nation. We contacted several ministries about connecting with them.

When we got to Timisoara, we found out they had been told that we were a rock and roll group. So, we moved out into the square and set up. Our preaching followed a group from Concord that was doing mime and breaking bricks. The people crowded around us by the hundreds and were listening as far as we could see in buildings all around. When we gave the altar call, hundreds of people knelt down in the square in 100-degree weather on the hard cobblestones for 20 minutes crying out to God.

One day, while we were out there, we tried to give out Bibles, which was a colossal mistake. The reporter who was with us stated it was a bigger riot than the revolution back in December. Five men got Moses Vegh in an arm lock and took all of his Bibles off him. People were swarming around on all sides. They ripped my shirt, pulled my hair and took all my Bibles.

They were on all four sides of the van rocking it back and forth, about to tip it over. All four of our Volkswagen vans were charged on Moses Vegh's American Express account. They were all damaged. One was smashed on all four sides, and the insurance company told us they wished we had left it on the side of the road because it would be worth more if it had been stolen.

The next day, suffice it to say, we did not give out Bibles but were aware of the fact that we needed an orderly plan to do so. People like Moses Vegh, who had been in 60 nations by that time and preached to tens of thousands of people, said he had never in his life seen such hunger for the Word.

During our last week in Romania, the pastors on our team were interviewed on the radio every hour on the hour in

Bucharest. This confirmed what we sensed Romania needed at that time, in order to be revitalized spiritually, economically and politically.

We travelled about 4000 miles by car in 18 days with the unlimited gas provided by the Communist Party. We ministered to several thousands of people, with close to 2000 decisions made for Christ. The trip was extremely difficult, and we were constantly subjected to changes of schedule, as some of the Romanian pastors were afraid of us. Others made promises they could not deliver, and others were just downright untruthful and their word was not any good. The thousands of decisions for Christ were obviously not a priority to them. We soon discovered that some of these traditional church leaders had only invited us in order to obtain money, medical supplies and resources, and to gain contacts in what they perceived to be the wealthy American church. After 41 years of oppression, that is how they survived.

We came to a point where we realized that God was in charge, and, frankly, we didn't need anybody's church, stadium or contacts. In some cases, they were a waste of time and a hindrance because we could set up almost anywhere. A whole new breed of intellectuals and professionals were ready to take leadership in the nation. Spiritually, they were ripe for training and preparation but could not be subjected to the bondage of the Pentecostal movement.

Among the crowd of people getting saved on our trip were doctors, lawyers, dentists, university students and many others. Ceausescu, despite the fact that he had the students recite that there was no God and that religion is a myth, had not been successful in stamping out the memory of God. The only thing he had done was create an intense, insatiable hunger for God. Those who were privileged to witness what God allowed to transpire on this trip have these scenes stamped forever on their psyche.

LESSON LEARNED: The great spiritual God-shaped vacuum in Romania had caused an insatiable hunger for something real and authentic. They were searching for something super-natural beyond themselves despite their unbelief, skepticism and distrust of all authorities, including God. As I was reviewing this life-changing experience, I could not help but think that we are living in a post-Christian era in America. There are few if any givens, absolutes or solid convictions. My prayer is that if God can revisit the nations in Eastern Europe, Asia and Africa, then I say, please, Lord, don't bypass us in America.

CHAPTER 32

Argentina

ONE OF THE GREATEST HINDRANCES TO WHAT GOD desires to do today is what He did yesterday. We all find security with the tried, proven, well-established and familiar pathways. We love to talk new and at the same time act old when it comes to pursuing the new faith walk upon which God would have us embark.

God is a God of infinite variety, and He is not limited or restricted to any one particular mode of operation. His principles remain consistent, but the methodology and technology are constantly evolving. Our natural tendency is to attempt to get God to repeat Himself, especially if we discover something that seems to be working successfully. Yet, Jesus never healed two people in the same manner. He would take some by the hand and raise them up; others He just walked by and never said a word. Jesus indicated to one that his sins were forgiven, and to still others He merely spoke the Word and healed them. Other times He put spit and mud in their eyes or told them to go and show themselves to the priest, who was the medical examiner at that time.

The greatest impeding force to the wave coming in on the ocean shore is the receding wave, which is heading back out to sea. Likewise, it is historically true that those who experienced the last revival become the most resistant toward what God is doing today. Consequently, every time God moves again, He has to raise up a brand-new group of people who are open to change because they are not totally vested in the past. These are people who refuse to build walls and say, "Thus far and no more." They are unwilling to drive their tent pegs down and remain in an unmovable, fossilized state.

A few years ago, I was asked to speak at the oldest Pentecostal church in Argentina. I was speaking about revival and God supernaturally visiting a nation. A pastor at the service took me aside and said, "I want to inform you that there is absolutely no revival in this nation. Regardless of what you have heard from Argentinian pastors who have gone to America talking about revival in this nation, it is not accurate." He added, "If there was a revival, it would be something that we would be very much aware of, and it would come through our church because we are the oldest Pentecostal church in the nation." Unfortunately, the majority of the people in the congregation were senior citizens.

That night we got into our car and drove a few miles down the road to a church that seated several thousand. It was a Friday night prayer meeting, and they had already turned away over a thousand people who were mostly college-aged, and who could not get into the building. This church was experiencing all kinds of signs, wonders and miracles on a regular basis.

Many churches, sadly, are going to be praying for revival all the way through the next revival. It could be happening all around them, and they are going to miss it. Jesus is recorded, in the New Testament, to have wept over Jerusalem for having tragically missed its brief window of opportunity.

For many of the faithful, this would be a once-in-a-lifetime season of miraculous visitation. As this will be totally unique to each individual, it therefore does not need to be cloned by anyone else.

This was vividly illustrated to me as a young boy when I was privileged to be an eyewitness to scores of authentic creative healing miracles. It was during the healing revivals of the '50s, when it was not unusual to see terminally ill people wheeled in on stretchers and then walk out on their own.

At nine years of age I traveled for 30 hours on the Canadian National Railway with my childhood friend Gordon and his mother, Margaret Shoemaker, from New Westminster, British Columbia, to Edmonton, Alberta. We were going to a William Branham meeting, which was held in a large downtown auditorium that seated about 20,000 people.

It was the middle of the day, and the building was totally packed. Mrs. Shoemaker was a rather quiet, humble, unassuming person who always radiated the presence of God. She had a large goiter on her throat. When we got into the arena, the service was already in progress, and William Branham was calling out sicknesses with a word of knowledge.

We had hardly gotten into the building when Branham stopped right in the middle of a sentence to begin praying for "Mrs. Shoemaker from New Westminster, who lived near the Pattullo Bridge." New Westminster was a rather small city at that time, located 1,500 miles from Edmonton, where we were. I remember my friend and I being quite skeptical, thinking that there must have been someone in the audience who knew her and gave her name to the evangelist. We soon realized that this was practically impossible given the large crowd, and no one had any foreknowledge of our being there.

The goiter shrank immediately. If I was not a believer before, I certainly became one at that very moment.

Humor in Ministry

LIFE LESSON I WAS NOT PREPARED FOR

I was taught that God was a good paymaster and that whenever you would sow where the people could not reciprocate, God would always faithfully, in turn, cause you to reap in places where you did not sow.

After ministering at a sizeable conference in the late '70s in Mexico, I was asked to go and speak at a rural church, which was located in a tiny remote village several miles off the paved road.

I had made a pledge to the Lord, when I began ministering, that I would always preach to a small crowd of 10 just as enthusiastically as I would to a crowd of 1,000. That night was to be no exception, and at the end of the service they took up a love offering for me and urged the people to give generously. They seemed to be so happy to give me the offering, which amounted to about $2 US. I politely refused it and gave it back to them for their church ministry.

The pastor became quite visibly offended, and he stated that this was the best that they had to give even though in an American way of thinking it was very small. He told me that this was equivalent to the widow's mite, and whether I knew it or not, I was literally robbing them of a huge blessing. At that moment, I felt tremendously embarrassed and humiliated. I realized that, although I had always considered myself to be a substantial giver, I was really a very poor receiver. I repented to the Lord and to the pastor and to the whole church and told them that they had taught me a very, very valuable lesson that night on being willing to receive regardless of their capacity to give.

Then to make matters worse they took up another offering to give me more!

CHAPTER 33

South Africa Racial Reconciliation

Iℕ Jᴏʜɴ 4:4, Jᴇsᴜs ᴍᴀᴅᴇ ᴛʜᴇ sᴛᴀᴛᴇᴍᴇɴᴛ ᴛᴏ Hɪs disciples, "And he must needs go through Samaria." As far as the disciples were concerned, they could have quite easily bypassed Samaria altogether, because there was great animosity between the Jews and the Samaritans. Developing committed relationships with people from different backgrounds and races doesn't just happen by accident. It can only happen when we are willing to repent of our overt attitudes and acts of discrimination that have fostered racial, gender and class separation, as well as denominational division. Every Christian of every race needs to experience a "must needs go through Samaria" excursion. Bishop Joseph Garlington has said that the church is the only institution on the face of the earth that can both proclaim and demonstrate what true biblical reconciliation looks like. Second Corinthians 5:18 states that the only ministry that each of us has in common is the ministry of reconciliation, and this is based on the fact that we have all been reconciled to Christ.

In the mid-'90s, my son and I made a trip to Durban, South Africa. I had been asked to speak at a large conference where several thousand people were in attendance from all over the

African continent, as well as many other nations. The general theme of the conference was Kingdom expansion through the releasing of apostolic and prophetic ministry. The sessions were all jam-packed with high-powered speakers, and there was an unusual outpouring of the Holy Spirit amidst some unfortunate controversial interjections, which challenged traditional theology. Grace prevailed, and God's purpose was accomplished in this monumental conference, which no doubt impacted several nations.

At the conclusion of this conference, they organized an outdoor youth concert. It was made up of a number of South African singers and bands, and it was held in a park in the center of the city. Several hundred interested youth gathered that day in what proved to be an amazing South African-style worship experience. We couldn't help but notice that as the concert began, there were three distinctly different groups that assembled. There were what they referred to as the Blacks, the Afrikaans and the Indians. They were all seated on the ground in three separate sections with at least 10–12 feet of separation between each group, and it was obvious they had no communication with each other. Even though they were all supposedly Christians from different churches. My son, Patrick, who was one of the speakers at the event, began addressing the crowd about the obvious division that existed at this concert. He reminded them that the laws of apartheid that kept people apart in the past had been banned in 1994 when Nelson Mandela became president. He stated that the church of Jesus Christ was a terrible witness to the world if we couldn't even get together in unity at a worship concert. So, he asked them to get up and move from their comfortably segregated sections, and join their brothers and sisters of other races and become fully integrated. He stated that they could now potentially form some brand new Christian friendships that could last a lifetime. He also suggested that they take their new friends back to their homes and introduce them to their families, which was something that rarely ever happened. After Patrick's request, something seemed to break loose in the atmosphere as we began to worship together. The spirit of reconciliation was present and powerfully demonstrated.

For several decades, our church in Oakland has miraculously maintained a diverse and united congregation, comprised of citizens from 50+ different nations. Our congregation has people from Central and South America, Asia (China, Japan and the Philippines), Africa and Europe as well as from different races from across America.

Shiloh pastors have always attempted to join hands across all racial and denominational barriers, and to work cooperatively to advance the Kingdom of God. They recognize that, with all our differences, we are still all part of the Body of Christ. We have also served on numerous boards and committees with the mayor and city council officials, law enforcement personnel, fire department personnel, public school administration and faculty and multiple social agencies. The goal has been to serve and improve the quality of life for every resident of our community and region.

The church of the 21st century must aggressively confront the two giants of sectarianism and racism, which are still alive and well, with love and action, lest we form our own brand of apartheid right here and now in our beloved America.

In Summary

All of the stories contained in this book were written in 2017, in between three intense surgical heart procedures. This gave me ample opportunity to consider the kind of legacy and inheritance, as Proverbs 13:22 says, that God had desired for me to leave to my children's children, both biological and spiritual. I concluded that my primary mission and goal in life is to fully utilize all of my spiritual giftings and resources to impart my values, passion, vision and faith to all those who are within my sphere of influence who are destined to outlive me. I

213

encourage you, as the reader, to allow your own personal story to unfold in order to fully discover, as I have, just how blessed, enriched and favored your life has been and it has only just begun.

CPSIA information can be obtained
at www.ICGtesting.com
Printed in the USA
FSOW02n2212281217
42240FS